THE
PICTURE
POSTCARD
& ITS ORIGINS

A drawing from the *Illustrated London News,* October 2, 1909. It is entitled "A Postcard Habit in Germany: the Postman as a walking Stationer and Letter-box". The caption reads: "The rage for picture postcards appears to be still the rage in Germany, as it is in this country. The people of Berlin want to write postcards even when sitting in an open-air restaurant. The cards the postman sells are written there and then, and promptly posted in the letter-box which he carries on his back."

THE
PICTURE
POSTCARD
& ITS ORIGINS

FRANK STAFF

Author of *The Penny Post 1680–1918*
and *The Transatlantic Mail*

LUTTERWORTH PRESS   LONDON

CONTENTS

FOREWORD TO NEW EDITION

When this book was first published in 1968, picture postcard collecting had been quietly pursued since the latter part of the 1950s and was a revival of the great collecting craze which was almost universal at the turn of the century, with collectors all over the world corresponding as 'pen-pals' and exchanging picture postcards. It was an interesting hobby and one that incurred little expense. The finest postcards published by the leading firms cost one penny or a few cents each. These were widely advertised and easily available to everyone.

During the 1960s, discriminating collectors had little difficulty in finding the sort of cards they wanted. There were plenty to be found at very little cost. One was guided by one's own interests while enjoying the pleasure and excitement in finding what one wanted.

It is perhaps amusing to note that at this time the same type of cards were looked for as in the 1900s; artistic designs, with the artist's signature, pictures of places and events, views of cities and towns, which today hold a nostalgic interest, and glamour in the form of pretty ladies, a taste for which remains unchanged.

In the 1970s, the remarkable appeal of picture postcard collecting grew to enormous proportions.

Postcard societies and clubs are now established all over U.S.A. and Britain, as well as in many other countries; the international demand produces catalogues and price lists in many languages which show the increasing values of popular and rare cards. Well-known auction houses of world repute sell postcards – singly and as collections under the hammer, when substantial prices are realized.

The picture postcard now enjoys a high reputation in the world of antiques and is today not always collected for its nostalgic or other interests, but for its potential value in an ever increasing market.

It is however fortunate that the early postcards pictured an endless variety of subjects and have recorded so much that might have been overlooked or forgotten, and it is still possible to enjoy a relatively cheap but nevertheless rewarding hobby by looking for little known features or variations on a theme.

FRANK W. STAFF

FOREWORD
by James Laver

Owing to the almost incurable human habit of taking things for granted, people are always astonished when they have laid before them the real history of some object of daily use, just as youngsters today find it difficult to believe that motor-cars, aeroplanes and television have not always been with us, so older people are astonished to learn that so common a thing as a postcard only came into being about the year 1870. We need someone like Mr. Frank Staff to spell out the story for us.

When one comes to think of it, it is obvious that post-cards could not have existed before the introduction of the penny post in 1840. But it needed a whole generation after that before their use was authorized. Even the name had to be invented, for when a prominent Post Office official of the North German Confederation first had the bright idea in 1865 he called his brain-child an *offenes Postblatt*. The Austrians were the first to take up the notion, and the world's first postcard came into being on October 1, 1869. Exactly a year later England followed suit.

Postcards, when first introduced, encountered an astonishing amount of opposition. Would not the servants read the messages? Would not people be insulted by a missive bearing only a ha'penny stamp? (They had not been insulted by the penny stamp on letters.) Fortunately no less a person than Gladstone adopted the new device, and soon there were so many cards in transit that the Post Office machinery was swamped.

Most of these were plain postcards, and Mr. Staff rightly draws attention to their effect on epistolary style. There was no room on a postcard for "long descriptive phrases and lengthy expressions of endearment". There was even less room when the cards became pictorial.

How this came about is a fascinating story. Germany was once more in the van with small views on a corner of the card of spas and other resorts, hotels and restaurants. The first use of the picture postcard seems to have been for purposes of publicity. The next step was easy, and during the subsequent decade the picture postcard as we know it was established in every civilized country in the world.

The great interest of Mr. Staff's book lies in the trouble he has taken to establish the ancestry of the picture post-card, and it is astonishing to learn how many lines of descent had to come together to make it possible. The trade cards of the seventeenth century, the visiting cards of the eighteenth century with their exquisite engravings, vignettes of cupids, musical instruments and the like, tradesmen's letter heads of the early nineteenth century, the pictorial writing paper of the 1850s and 1860s and, of course, the famous Mulready envelope which provoked so much ridicule. All this Mr. Staff expounds with immense learning and conscientiousness.

Once established, the picture postcard soon began to reflect every facet of human nature. There were (following the old tradition) views of pleasure resorts and foreign places intended to impress the recipient, sentimental cards, patriotic cards and even (sad to say) "obscene" cards—the authorities soon clamped down on these, but seem to have turned a blind eye on the "vulgar" cards which still embellish the windows of every shop selling seaside souvenirs —immensely fat women bursting out of their bodices or leaning provocatively over the railings of the promenade. Well! well! An outmoded vulgarity has its own "period charm".

The craze for collecting cards seems to have begun in the 1890s. Even Queen Victoria is said to have been affected by it, and soon no "drawing room table" was complete without one of the special albums in which picture postcards could be preserved. They took the place of the "family albums" of photographs dear to the previous generation. Perhaps the years between 1895 and 1914 saw the heyday of the picture postcard. The short message is now more conveniently conveyed by the telephone. And, after all, if the cost of sending a letter has only risen by 400 per cent., the cost of sending a postcard has risen by 600 per cent. How shocked Gladstone—and George Bernard Shaw—would have been by that!

Mr. Staff's book will be welcomed not only by collectors, but by anyone interested in those trivia of the past which often shed more light on social developments than the most pretentious treatise. It is exactly such a footnote to history that the picture postcard provides.

INTRODUCTION

Picture postcards are such commonplace items of everyday use that few people ever bother to consider why or how they ever came into existence. Yet like everything else, they had a beginning, and this book gives the story of what is known of their origins and early uses.

The postcard was not invented. It evolved, and with its creation the writing habits of the civilized world were completely changed. Adding a picture to a postcard was a natural sequel and happened as a matter of course.

These early artistic efforts are not only of great interest from the point of view of printing and art, but give pleasure to all who look at them, quite apart from a certain amount of amusement which many of them sometimes unintentionally give.

Today, sending a picture postcard to friends and relations is often the easiest and most convenient means of keeping in touch, and many a friendship has been maintained or saved by this simple expedient.

Collecting old picture postcards is of absorbing interest. The detail and unusual items of domestic and social history which they show are of inestimable value to the historian. Street scenes and places of note in our cities and towns have become so changed in recent years either as a result of destruction in the last war, or by reason of development and rebuilding, as to be hardly recognizable when seen on postcards of fifty years ago, consequently these are of great service as social records.

Our conception of art, beauty and humour contrasts sharply with what was depicted on postcards of fifty years ago and sometimes nostalgic memories are revived whenever an old-time postcard album is looked through.

Ephemeral bygones—especially those of paper—are the sort most liable to get destroyed, but thanks to the acquisitiveness and the collecting instinct in man, many are saved to become cherished items of a collection, to be enjoyed and admired sometimes by those same people who, out of ignorance and indifference, had, years before, thrown them out!

For the help they have given me in one form or another I am indebted to:

F. E. Dixon of Rathgar, Dublin.
Ben Shiffrin of New York.
Charles A. Fricke of Philadelphia.
Mirko Verner of Novi Sad, Jugoslavia.
Franz Hutter of Melk, Austria.
Messrs. Pierre Langlois and Jean Pothion of Paris.
P. Schoenmann of Cardiff.
A. W. Morley of Manchester, and
Norman Shepherd of Poole.

I am also obliged to Mr. Thomas of the G.P.O. Records Room, to the assistants of the library in the Victoria and Albert Museum, and to the Oxford University Press for allowing me to visit the John Johnson Collection of Ephemeral Printing.

I am also grateful for assistance and advice given to me by Mr. A. L. M. Valentine of Messrs. Valentine and Sons Ltd., Dundee, Messrs. Bamforth and Co. Ltd., and to Mr. C. W. Hayes of Messrs. Raphael Tuck and Sons Ltd., who have kindly allowed the reproduction of some of their cards. Lastly, to the Proprietors of *The Illustrated London News* for permission to reproduce the interesting picture as the frontispiece.

FRANK W. STAFF.

West Bay, Bridport.

1. A postcard of 1900. (Slightly reduced)

1

EARLY PICTORIAL CARDS

PEOPLE have always liked to draw pictures; evidence exists all over the world of attempts made by primitive man since earliest times to set down on stone, or on bone or shell, the things he has seen. Usually his pictures are decorative, and this urge to beautify would seem to be inherent. Even a child, when given crayons and paper, will make some efforts to draw the things he knows and will cover his paper with some sort of a design, so that this must surely be a natural tendency in man.

Long before the invention of paper, drawings were made on whatever was considered a suitable surface, and many of these being of a hard durable substance have fortunately been preserved. The subjects depicted seem for the most part to have been portraits—much the same in fact as any small child will attempt when given the opportunity. That these artistic efforts were given by way of a present, from one to another, can be assumed without much fear of contradiction, and it can be reasonably established that giving a picture was one of the earliest known forms of a gift, in much the same way as a small toddler proudly gives to its mother a piece of scribbling. Man, although rough, cruel and often heartless, will somehow or other find the time, when given the chance, to create something "pretty". Prisoners of war, although hardened by all the horrors of their experience, will write or draw something charming or beautiful to help while away the time in captivity. Seamen too, especially the whalers of the last century, with time to spare on their long voyages, have given us proof of how they spent their leisure by the fascinating and often beautifully designed "scrimshaw" work—little pictures scratched or carved on pieces of bone or the tusks of animals. The following lines serve as a pleasant reminder of this sort of pastime:

Accept dear girl, this busk from me
Carved by my humble hand.
I took it from a sperm whale's jaw
One thousand miles from land.
In many a gale Had been the whale,
In which this bone did rest.
His time is past, His bone at last
Must now support thy breast.

Doodling, too, is quite a pastime for many, and the designs which come by chance in such an uncontrolled way show that there is a creative instinct at work.

The monks and scribes who wrote the psalms and missals so painstakingly were rarely content to leave the vellum pages without some form of decoration, and are responsible for designs over the lines or in the embellishment of the capital letters, which have often been executed in most elaborate and beautiful styles. The monks too, sometimes, "doodled" on their work. An example in the writer's collection shows fishes dangling at the ends of some of the twirls and flourishes, and in another, little faces are cunningly drawn in some of the loops and ovals of the smaller letters. This sort of decorated page, common in the Middle Ages, can be considered the prototype of the ornamental writing paper of a much later date, which became fashionable during the first part of the 19th century and which has again become popular in recent years, especially in our modern "notelets".

With the invention of printing on paper, it was a natural sequence to have illustrations and drawings printed in books. Following printed books, all sorts of printing came to be decorated, sometimes slightly, sometimes lavishly. Tradespeople, when printing their billheads, used decoration. In the 17th century the designs were fairly simple, but as the 18th century advanced, highly decorative and beauti-

2. A visiting card, circa 1770–80. This view of the Fountain of Moses is still to be seen in Rome. (Actual size)

3. A visiting card, circa 1770–80, showing the Piazza Signoria, Florence. (Actual size)

ful printing resulted. The engraving on these so-called trade cards reached a height of perfection, and the designs invariably included the picture of the sign under which the business flourished, as well as the type of goods sold.

It was about now that playing cards (which had come to England sometime during the 15th century by way of France and Italy) were sometimes used as visiting cards,[1] by having the name of the caller written across the blank reverse, quite an ancient custom. By the mid-18th century visiting cards were being manufactured on the Continent. Their size conformed more or less to the usual size of a playing card, and an ornamental frame of tasteful design surrounded the edge, leaving the centre blank for the name to be written on. Very soon visiting cards were printed showing pictures, sometimes in classical style, but often depicting actual views, favourite topics being the ruins of antiquities. As a rule they were delicately engraved, with sufficient space left somewhere in the design for the name to be written in; but it was only a short step to include the name of the person, and privately printed cards all had the names engraved on them.

With a stretch of the imagination it could be said that these pictorial visiting cards are the direct ancestors of the picture postcard, especially when it is remembered that messages were sometimes written on them. Continental examples are known, too, bearing a written New Year's greeting, so that they can also be considered as the forerunner of greetings cards.

In 1777 a French engraver in Paris named Demaison published engraved cards with greetings on them to be sent through the local "penny post", but the idea was not popu-

[1] *Connoisseur*, April 1905, "Old Artistic Visiting Cards".

lar because, not being enclosed under cover, the messages could be read by servants and others through whose hands they passed.

Visiting cards were published and sold in sets, printed or engraved as a rule on stout paper or thin card, in the form of sheets, showing eight little pictures to be cut out as required. Possibly some were sold already cut, but this will not be known for certain, unless some chance mention of the sale of such objects is found one day in a contemporary letter or book of the period. In the old antiquarian print shops of Rome it is still possible to find sheets of these visiting cards, but it is probable that these sheets, such as are offered today, although genuinely engraved in the 18th century, are samples or proofs, for they are printed on much thinner paper than was customary for the ordinary visiting cards of the day. Sold in this shape they might have been intended for the purpose of pasting into scrap albums.

France, Italy and Austria seem to be the countries where most of the early pictorial visiting cards were published, but British examples compare equally well with Continental work. Often charmingly designed and elegantly engraved, they sometimes showed landscapes and beautiful little views of the estates of the nobility and landed gentry. Looking over a collection of these old cards, there will usually be found one or two of Continental manufacture inscribed with English names. It is possible that cards were purchased by English visitors when travelling abroad; quite recently one of a series of cards, delicately engraved with a view of the Piazza Signoria, Florence, showing the Loggia dei Lanzi and bearing the name of "Mrs. Chase", was found in an old bookshop in London. This is an identical design to another card which was obtained in Rome, showing the Pitti Palace of Florence, with the written name of "Il Conte Sgrinfia". Such cards, prettily decorated and of foreign origin, would doubtless enhance the personal ego of the owner when brought back to England.

The very high standard of workmanship seen on many of these 18th-century visiting cards indicates that they were done by the best artists of the day. Indeed, famous engravers did not consider the work beneath them, and sometimes, but not frequently, the artist's signature shows on the card.

It was around this period too, the latter part of the 18th century, that British trade cards—cards issued by the proprietors of every conceivable sort of business—were highly ornamental. The type of pictorial advertisement, elaborately engraved with a lengthy description of everything the merchant had for sale, on the blank side of which it was customary to write the bill, had by now become a tradesman's billhead, as we know it today; except that it was headed as a rule by elegant engravings. In addition, the tradesman or

4. Trade card of 1764. These cards were often used as bills, items being listed on the back. (Actual size)

SECOND-HAND PLATE

WATCHES & JEWELS.

Briscoe & Morrison,

JEWELLERS and GOLDSMITHS,

at the Old Shop

the three KINGS and GOLDEN BALL

Opposite Foster Lane in Cheapside,

1764

LONDON

Continues to Make it their particular Business,

to Deal in all Sorts of

New and Second Hand Plate, Watches and Jewels,

of which they have constantly the greatest Variety and are

determin'd to Sell (as formerly) at Lower Prices than Common

and Likewise to Give the most Money for any Quantities of

Old Plate, Watches, Jewels, Pearls, & Colour'd-stones of all Kinds,

by reason of the great Demand they have for y'e Same.

N.B. The full Value Given for Pawn'd Plate, Watches, Jewels &c.

BUY AND SELL FOR READY MONEY ONLY.

11

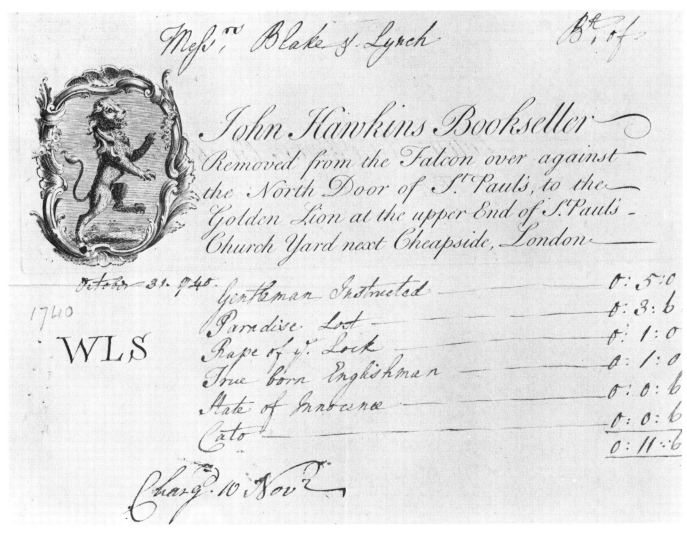

Mess.rs Blake & Lynch

Bt. of

John Hawkins Bookseller
Removed from the Falcon over against
the North Door of St Paul's, to the
Golden Lion at the upper End of St Paul's
Church Yard next Cheapside, London

October 31. 1740. Gentleman Instructed		0 : 5 : 0
Paradise Lost		0 : 3 : 6
Rape of ye Lock		0 : 1 : 0
True born Englishman		0 : 1 : 0
State of Innocence		0 : 0 : 6
Cato		0 : 0 : 6
		0 : 11 : 6

1740

WLS

Charg. 10 Nov.r

5. Tradesman's bill of 1740. Note the prices and the books listed. (Actual size)

merchant used a card in size usually conforming to the size of a playing card. These trade cards have in recent years become more and more difficult to find, and are eagerly sought after by collectors of this kind of ephemera.

By reason of the excellence of their engraving and the style and decoration of their design, they have a charm all their own, and were keenly collected many years ago, so that specimens today will turn up only by chance. But unlike visiting cards, they can hardly be associated in the same way as ancestors of picture postcards, for they were never sold in sets and were never published for sale. They do, however, have a connection in so far as they are pictorial and were intended to "attract the eye", by reason of the high quality of their printing, the beauty of their design and their overall charm. They are essentially, however, advertisements.

Visiting cards of foreign origin of the latter part of the 18th century frequently showed places of historic interest and famous monuments, but, as well as these, cards were published showing motifs of a very general nature, so that they suited the tastes of everyone. These visiting cards in fact were subject to the same influence which was brought to bear at a much later date on picture postcards. The demand for novelty led to series after series, not only of views of different towns and places of antiquity, but also of reproductions of works of art, maps of countries and districts, geometrical ornaments, and even some which featured playing cards, which might be likened to the old custom of using playing cards with names written on the backs.

As might be expected, not everyone wanted made-to-order cards, but many people liked to show their individual interests by using cards which showed their professions or occupations. A card of the archivist, Signor Rivaroli, shows him in his room attending to a caller, surrounded by piles of documents and papers upon shelves. In the space below his counter is written (by hand) "L. Rivaroli Archivista". An interesting card of the Marchese Guiseppe Ginori depicts him in the act of paying a call; his carriage, drawn by two fine horses, with attendant coachmen, is shown turning in the road before the portal of a town house, towards which a footman is hastening to hand his master's card to a servant waiting in the doorway. A similarly designed card in the author's collection was used by Prince Lambertini, which might indicate that this was a fashionable design available to the aristocracy.

For those holding a commission in the army or in some way connected with the Service there were cards embellished with swords, cannon, flags and all the insignia of a military nature, sometimes showing a figure in uniform. Two such cards in the author's collection are hand-coloured, but whether coloured at a later date in order to decorate a scrap book or a family album will never be known. Many of these early cards were printed not only in black, but in sepia, green or blue, and as several are sometimes found in colour it is quite possible that this was consistent with the fashion of the day.

It was because of the beauty and charm of these little picture cards that so many have been saved. For they were kept as souvenirs, to be put into the family album; maybe those having the names of distinguished and noble persons were intended to impress whoever might glance over the pages. It is certainly thanks to the people of those days saving such commonplace objects in their albums that so many of these delightful little works of art are still preserved. These cards with their pictures and decorated designs were kept in much the same way as people saved picture postcards just over a hundred years later.

With the turn of the century, the style and design of visiting cards changed. They were no longer pictorial; the fashion was for smaller cards with the name engraved boldly in large copperplate. Occasionally the background would be gilded over an embossed design, otherwise any decoration there might be was much simpler. Among the nobility, a popular fashion was to have an elaborately engraved monogram, with the full name showing along the twirls and twists of the letters.

In Austria, about this time, many cards were heavily embossed with a decorative design, often showing a person, sometimes two, male and female gracefully posed; somewhere in the design a small panel would be left blank for the name to be filled in.

But, with pictorial visiting cards about to go out of fashion, writing paper, which over the centuries had remained quite plain, now began to be decorated.

The process was very gradual, and probably started in France and Italy, when writing paper with a decorated

6. Engraved on heavy paper, this 'trade card' also served as the tradesman's bill, the amount being written on the back. Dated 1736. (Slightly reduced)

7. A carrier's trade card, circa 1800. (Slightly reduced)

8. Eighteenth-century visiting card, one of a set of 12, showing monthly occupations. (Actual size)

9. Visiting card, published in Rome 1788, of a military design. (Actual size)

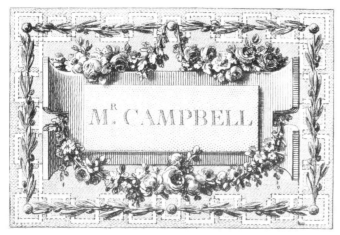

10. An English visiting card, circa 1790. (Actual size)

border of hand-coloured flowers and leaves came on the market sometime about the 1780s. Examples in the author's collection dated 1790 have the appearance of being stencilled, and show costumed figures of a lady on one sheet and a gentleman on the other, each positioned in a different place on the page.

It is very probable that this form of decoration had its beginnings when people, travelling in a foreign country, would write home to their families and friends, and in order to explain better some particular description in the letter, would embellish the pages with a sketch or water-colour, illustrating some aspect of national costume or an historical monument they had seen on the journey.

With the advent of the French revolution, France now led the way by having the writing paper of the many new government offices and departments headed with the cap of liberty, and sometimes quite lavishly emblazoned with the motif of Liberty, Equality and Fraternity, often beautifully engraved; many of these, which are usually foolscap size, show a high standard of printing, especially those produced during the Napoleonic régime for the occupied countries of Italy and Switzerland. The pictorial letter headings used in Switzerland show for the most part William Tell with his son, or else the taking of the Rütli oath, which brought about the original Swiss Con-federation.

A few years later, Napoleon's soldiers and sailors were able to write home on paper headed by engraved pictures of a military or naval flavour, showing mounted dra-goons, soldiers handling their weapons, and warships. They can be said to be the earliest known patriotic stationery. Sometimes they are to be found hand coloured, and the fact that they are very scarce denotes that not many soldiers could afford this luxury. For, although large quantities of soldiers' and sailors' letters written throughout the Napoleonic wars have been pre-served, not many examples of this sort of ornamental writing paper exist, and collectors are keen to find them.

Another type of pictorial writing paper which was making its appearance about this time, common in many countries, was that used by the better class tradesmen and shopkeepers, who headed their note-paper with a pictorial representation of their business. Such note-paper was frequently used for the rendering of accounts, and is to be found whenever any accumulation of old corre-spondence or family papers turns up.

In Italy, pictorial writing paper was now appearing headed by the same engravings formerly used for visiting cards, the publishers using the same blocks, and making little effort to conceal the fact, for examples are some-times found showing the blank space intended for a

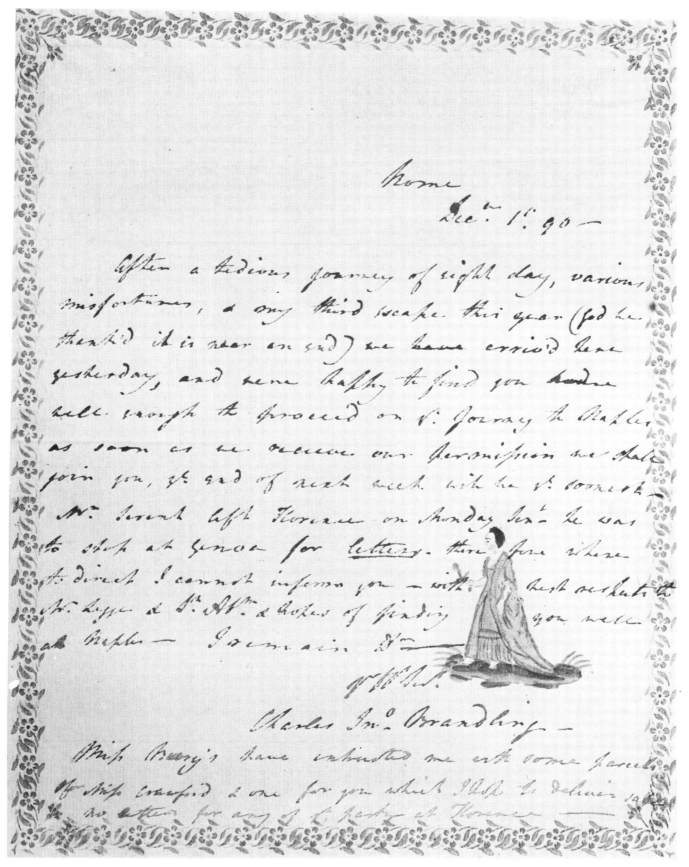

Rome
Decr 1st 90 —

After a tedious journey of eight days, various
misfortunes, & my third escape this year (God be
thank'd it is near an end) we arrived here
yesterday, and were happy to find you —
well enough to proceed on y.^r Journey to Naples
as soon as we receive our permission we shall
join you, y.^e end of next week will be y.^e soonest —
M.^r ____ left Florence on Monday ____ he was
to stop at Genoa for letters — therefore where
to direct I cannot inform you — with ____ best respects to
M.^r ____ & Sr W.^m & hopes of finding ____ you well
at Naples — I remain &.^c

y.^r M.st M.^t

Charles Ino. Brandling —

Miss Berry's have entrusted me with some parcels
& Miss Crawford & one for you which I shall be delivering to
the ____ letters for any I shall party at Florence ——

11. Printed in pink and green and dated 1790. Specimens of eighteenth-century ornamental writing paper are rare. (Actual size)

15

person's name. This therefore establishes a definite link between the pictorial visiting card and pictorial writing paper, and makes them both the ancestors of the picture postcard of a century later.

When finally the long wars with the French were ended, quite perceptibly an age of elegance emerged which has ever since marked the Regency period as years of especial grace and charm. The early Victorian era followed, referred to by German-speaking people by the comfortable German word *Biedermeyer*, a period which carries through to the 1860s or thereabouts, by which time the French were enjoying the glamorous years of the second Empire. These years saw, among other things, the commonplace articles of daily life made to look pretty, and this was especially so with many things of an ephemeral nature that were printed, such as invitation cards and tickets of all sorts; trade cards, bills, various little containers and covers, and writing paper and envelopes.

Quite early in the new century, a good quality writing paper made its appearance in England. It came in two sizes, quarto and octavo, and was double paged. This writing paper was sometimes headed with a beautifully embossed ornamental design, which often extended around the edges as well, and was sometimes adorned with a coloured border. Writing paper of this sort was popularly used for special occasions such as invitations, greetings and social events, and above all for St. Valentine's Day. A fine example in the author's collection which is on paper with a watermark dated 1814 is heavily embellished with patriotic motifs symbolizing the glories of the Allied victories and was evidently published to celebrate the victory of Waterloo. On the Continent, German-speaking countries favoured similar writing paper which was sometimes decorated in colour, and often adorned with dainty costumed figures. About this time too, in Germany, note-paper heavily ornamented with colourful designs, and corresponding in size to our modern

12. Engraved and hand-coloured, this type of headed notepaper was popularly used by French soldiers and sailors during the Napoleonic wars. (Actual size)

13. Very early English headed writing paper, dated 1832. (Slightly reduced)

notelets, came on the market, complete with a shaped flap ready for folding, so that no envelope was required.

Elsewhere, in most European countries, came the fashion for writing paper to be headed with an engraved view of the place or resort showing where the writer was staying. These were lithographed or engraved in such a beautiful way that they were seldom thrown away, but were usually cut from the letter and stuck into the family scrap album.

This fashion for headed note-paper might have started in Italy, where about the year 1830, as previously mentioned, writing paper was published headed with the same little views that were formerly printed on visiting cards. Soon, the whole top of the sheet came to be adorned by a panoramic view or landscape. A delightful example, which is printed in colour and dated 1832, bears the caption "South View of Worthing taken at Sea", and shows the whole stretch of the sea-front, with the leading hotels. In minute lettering along the bottom of the picture is: "Drawn & pub^d. by Ja^s. Rouse, Fulham for A. Carter, Library, 12 War-

wick St. Worthing, where may be had all the interesting Views & Antiquities of Sussex adapted for Scrap Books &c." Inside, on the second page of the letter, the writer has written "I hope you are amused at my writing paper. I keep the back free from writing in case you should like to cut the print off for a Scrap book or collection."

It is because of this habit of cutting out the picture that complete examples of these delightful souvenirs are so hard to find postally used; whereas unused specimens in almost new condition are not so difficult to obtain. This is because so many people during the Victorian era collected unused copies and bound them into book form. In this way, apart from quantities of unsold stock, many have been preserved. It is a great pity that because of their delicate beauty some modern booksellers sometimes colour them, and although they are delightful to look at, they lack their original charm, by being made to look too new.

Most examples of the early decorated embossed writing paper have been saved because they were used as Valentines.

14. A letter dated July 13, 1825 on English-made note-paper watermarked 1811. A good example of embossing. (Actual size)

My dear Madam

Very many thanks are due to you for your most obliging researches. Before I speak of the Kederminster family I must write of those which most interest us.

None deserved to be more esteemed or beloved than Dr Swabey by myself, and Mrs Cresswell. I lament that he is so great a sufferer, but his life is a blessing, and we must rejoice that he had health otherwise, and spirits. The studious man will live cheerfully where the mere gentleman will pine in misery and regret. The Christian with an eye steadily fixed upon Eternity, seldom greatly repines at dispensations. May your honoured father live long and have no farther illness. Please, Madam, to present my sincerest good wishes and compliments to Dr & Mrs Swabey, and to Mr Freeman and accept the same from me, & mine.

A visit from You and any others of the Family will confer a great obligation upon us.

I do not mention the state of health here, because I presume Mrs Cresswell has already written upon the subject.

Every family has an undoubted right to pronounce and spell the name as they please. The Kederminsters wrote theirs as you kindly inform me, but in the English Baronetage and Irish Peerage the orthography is Kidderminster.

I shall love my beautiful drawing the better for the history of Kederminsters having been elucidated by your pen. I request that Mr Freeman, and the curate of Langley will accept my best thanks. They have been very attentive to my inquisitiveness.

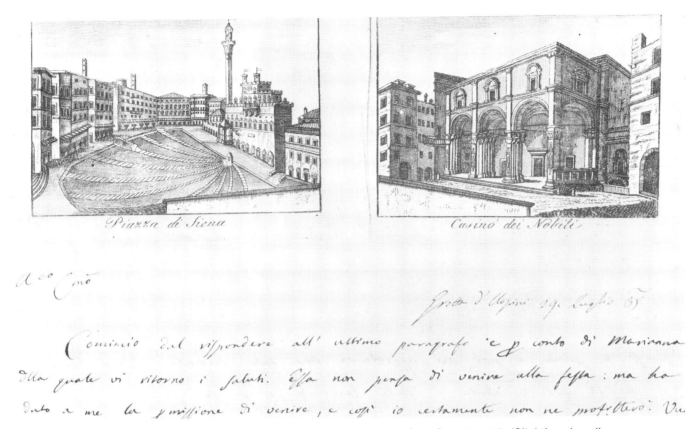

15. Pictorial visiting cards printed as a heading to writing paper. Postmarked from Siena in 1835. (Slightly reduced)

In North America, the giving of ornamental keepsakes, designed and decorated by hand, seems to have been far more prevalent than was the case in Britain, for several American examples are known, dated in the middle of the 18th century.

The ancient festival of St. Valentine's Day is the original survival of the festival of the Lupercalia which was introduced into Britain by the Romans, when, among other customs appertaining to the mating season, young men drew for the names of young women and paired-off. This festival of the Lupercalia was held during the month of February and, due to the martyrdom of an unfortunate Roman bishop named Valentinus who was cruelly clubbed to death on February 14 during the celebration of the Lupercalia, the early Christian Church, in reorganizing the calendar of festival days by substituting the names of Christian Saints for the pagan names, allocated February 14 to St. Valentine. Ever after, throughout the centuries, the wilder and more licentious behaviour and customs associated with the Lupercalia became tamed and more gentle, until it was only customary to bestow a present upon one's wife or lady friend—a popular gift being gloves or garters, and one which is frequently mentioned in old accounts and

references of this Saint's Day. Pepys in his diary mentions drawing for one's Valentine amongst friends, and giving presents to his wife. It was allowed also for married women to be kissed by their male friends, with the complete understanding and consent of their husbands—a sure survival of the ancient festival of the Lupercalia. It was common practice throughout the British Isles for young men to draw by lot the names of young women, a custom which lingered on in a few remote country places until Victorian times. By the end of the 18th century it was now becoming usual to send a keepsake in the shape of a lover's knot, or a lovingly written letter to one's lady friend or wife, and early in the 19th century these prettily inscribed verses were being written on the new-fashioned writing paper which was daintily ornamented with embossing all around, and the pages suitably decorated for the occasion with classical designs of little cupids.

One of the earliest manufacturers of this embossed writing paper was H. Dobbs, who began as a paper manufacturer at No. 8 New Bridge Street, London, in 1803. His business grew steadily, and in 1851 was known as Dobbs, Kidd and Company, regarded as one of the leading manufacturers of this type of ornamental paper. Today, Valen-

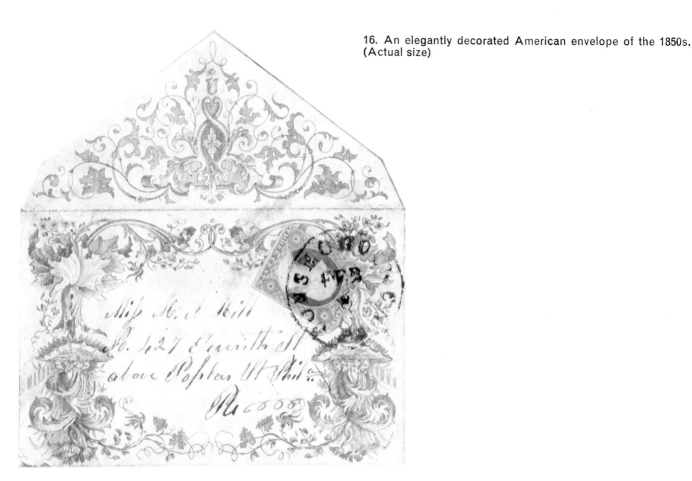

tines, as well as ornamental writing paper, bearing the name of Dobbs are highly prized among collectors.

Dobbs had many competitors, all producing this embossed paper of a very high quality, so that these English manufacturers became noted abroad for this sort of work. In great demand were the Valentine designs, and during the 1840s and 1850s these were shipped in considerable quantity to North America, as well as to the principal Colonies.

It should be remembered that prior to 1840, when a uniform penny postage was introduced, ordinary rates of postage were very high and were graded by distance and the number of sheets of paper forming the letter, so that Valentines could not be so conveniently and cheaply sent by post, consequently not many are to be found these days in a postally used condition, for it should also be borne in mind that envelopes were not yet in general use; Valentines which were to be posted conformed to the usual quarto sized letter sheet, and were folded, sealed, and then addressed. It follows also that such Valentines, and indeed any sort of ornamental paper, were used for the most part only by that section of the public able to afford such luxuries. This is one other reason why pictorial writing paper—and any sort of decorated writing paper postally used before 1840—is comparatively rare.

During the 1830s in England, quarto sized pictorial headed writing paper, showing views, was available in all the major cities, seaside resorts, and places of note.

These lithographed and engraved views usually depicted scenes differing from the many sets of views commonly available in the print shops and were therefore all the more popular. They were drawn by good artists and many were printed from the stone by the well-known C. Hullmandel. Usually they showed the name of the artist, the engraver and the publisher. From an examination of a quantity of these letter sheets all dated in the 1830s it appears that Dobbs and Company, and J. and F. Harwood of 26 Fenchurch Street, London, were the principal publishers of this sort of writing paper, although many local publishers in the provinces also produced excellent work.

The pictures often showed extremely realistic scenes such as a busy street crowded with horsedrawn traffic and shoppers; or a street market with its several groups of traders; a drover, walking slowly along a country road with his cattle, and busy harbour views, as well as the seaside pictures of little groups of people enjoying the seashore against a background of bathing machines being pulled by horses. They were on sale as a rule at the library, which, in all seaside towns and holiday resorts, was one of the most important places to visit. The library was a rendezvous for appointments. Here, ladies could show off

17. This example of notepaper is to be found in many colours with the views of Continental cities engraved boldly in black. Period 1840-50. (Actual size)

18. Quarto size letter heading published by Harwood of London in 1840. (Actual size)

their dresses (and comment on other people's). A vast assortment of things were on sale, such as souvenirs, knick-knacks, pictorial and fancy stationery, and sweetmeats. Raffles could be subscribed to, and the latest comic and romantic songs could be listened to. Charles Dickens has given us a good description of a library of this period at Ramsgate:

The library was crowded. . . . There were young ladies, in maroon-coloured gowns and black velvet bracelets, dispensing fancy articles in the shop, and presiding over games of chance in the concert-room. There were marriageable daughters, and marriage-making mammas, gaming and promenading, and turn-ing over music, and flirting. There were some male beaux doing the sentimental in whispers, and others doing the ferocious in moustache. There was Mrs. Tuggs in amber, Miss Tuggs in sky blue, Mrs. Captain Waters in pink. There was Captain Waters in a braided surtout; there was Mr. Cymon Tuggs in pumps and a gilt waistcoat; there was Mr. Joseph Tuggs in a blue coat and a shirt frill.

By the time Queen Victoria came to the throne in 1837, people bought this pictorial writing paper and used it in just the same way that people buy picture postcards today. But it was not for everyone; only for those who could afford it.

2

PICTORIAL ENVELOPES

IN 1840 an important development took place in the postal system of the British Isles which was to alter for ever the everyday life of the people. This was the introduction of a uniform penny postage, brought about after a hard struggle with autocratic postal officials and an apathetic government, by the efforts of Rowland Hill, backed by a substantial section of the general public, and in particular by the leading business men of the day. On January 10, 1840, a uniform rate of one penny per half ounce was charged for a letter anywhere within the Realm. With this great innovation, many people wrote letters who seldom had written before. For the price of one penny it was now possible to contact one's friends and relations quickly and cheaply. Greetings were exchanged between friends by post—and St. Valentine's Day was now celebrated as never before. Thanks also to the new postal reforms, the public were made acquainted with envelopes—sometimes described as "paper pockets".

Until the advent of penny postage, it was not possible to use an envelope without paying a double postage, because postal rates before 1840 were calculated on distance and per sheet of paper, and no matter how small or light a small piece of paper might be inside the smallest of envelopes, the letter was automatically rated a double postage.

Most of the envelopes were used by those privileged with the right of sending or receiving letters free, such as members of both Houses of Parliament and some public officials.

Now, with the coming of postage at the flat rate, envelopes were used by many people for the first time, and proved very popular.

The first envelopes sold by the Post Office were for use only from the Houses of Parliament, when free franking ceased on January 9, 1840. When the famous "Penny Black" postage stamp was put on sale early in May of the same year, it was accompanied also by a penny pre-paid envelope. There was also a twopenny envelope printed in blue. As well as being made in the form of envelopes, they were prepared also as covers, to be folded. They were ungummed, with open flaps, which had to be fastened by sealing wax or little paper wafers (envelopes were first issued gummed and with an adhesive flap in 1845). These Post Office envelopes bore a design excellently drawn by the well-known Royal Academician, William Mulready. The design was symbolical of a cheap and beneficial postage and showed Britannia with a lion at her feet, sending forth messengers to all quarters of the world, while merchants

19. Caricature of a Mulready envelope, comprising one of a set published by Spooner and used in July 1840. (Reduced)

20. Comic note-paper heading of the early 1840s published by Harris Bros. of London and printed in colour. Compare this with the postcard shown on page 78 (No. 123). (Reduced)

of all nationalities and people at home received their letters. It was a very fine artistic effort, but the public did not like it, and Mulready's envelope was ridiculed right from the start. In no time, enterprising publishers printed rude caricatures of Mulready's design, which appealed to the public's sense of humour.

First on the market was an envelope published by Fores of 41 Piccadilly, drawn by John Leech.

Inscribed along the top is "FORES' COMIC ENVELOPE NO. 1", an indication that others were to follow in a series, but apparently these did not materialize. Along the bottom of the envelope is printed in very small print: "London, Published by Messrs. Fores, at their Sporting & Fine Print Repository & Frame Manufactury 41 Piccadilly—corner of Sackville Street".

Thomas White, of 59 Wych Street, Strand, published two comic caricatures which cleverly burlesqued the original Mulready design, while another early issue of note was put out by William Spooner of 377 Strand. This firm had a reputation for humorous prints and paper novelties and was well known for the series of "Transformations" published during the 1830s.[1] Their series of fourteen comic envelopes was one of the most popular of this time, though the drawings could hardly be considered pleasant. With the exception of Nos. 13 and 14 in this set, all of them portrayed skits on sporting scenes, postal matters, courtship and flirting, writing, and all manner of everyday items. Britannia

was always shown looking like a fat old harridan, the lion at her feet was comical, and in one instance replaced by a donkey. The many figures which adorned the envelopes, although comical, had ugly faces, cunning expressions, leering looks, but were cleverly drawn and full of life. No. 8 in the set even went so far as lese-majesty. Queen Victoria is shown "in the family way", while next to her is her mother, the Duchess of Kent, saying, "De Brince sall be very useful at de rocking de cradle". To which the Queen replies, "Oh yes, he'll be very useful in time". Britannia with a broad grin on her face is pointing her spear towards Prince Albert who, rocking an empty cradle is saying, "Ah mine Loaf vat you tink I improve". Above him is written, "England expects every man to do his duty". Two other figures dressed as nurses—probably intended to represent Lord Melbourne and Lord Morpeth—complete the picture. A few of these envelopes carry the imprint: W. Mullheaded, as though to leave no doubt that they were satirizing William Mulready.

It might well be wondered why the well-drawn Mulready envelope with its appropriate design was shouted down by all and sundry. Articles and letters written about it in the daily press were strongly abusive and reflect all the more

[1] Transformations were prints, comic and otherwise, which were backed by coloured tissue. When held up to the light, the picture became quite changed. Picture postcards made as transparencies and "hold-ups" were hailed as novelties when they came on the market in the early 1900s.

24

the nature of these rude caricatures. But not all were rude. Nos. 13 and 14 of the Spooner series were cleverly drawn satires of political problems of the day. One of these refers to the alliance with Austria and the war in Syria, Britain being represented by Sir Charles Napier; the other is devoted to Daniel O'Connor who is shown balancing a Roman Catholic priest in his right hand and a trembling mannikin, intended to represent Lord Melbourne, in his left. All around the designs are other persons caricatured in association with problems of Ireland.

Similar in many ways to the Spooner series, though not quite so robust, was another set, six in all, with the imprint along the bottom of each envelope, "Published by J. W. Southgate, Library, 164 Strand" followed by a date. On the lower flap in an oblong panel is inscribed: REJECTED DESIGN'S (sic) FOR THE POSTAGE ENVELOPE. The six designs were issued on different dates during June 1840 and are all mildly amusing; of exceptional interest is No. 5 of the series which is wholly Dickensian in concept, for all the characters portrayed are clearly associated with Mr. Pickwick.

These early caricatures of Mulready's work are particularly interesting for the reason that they were the first pictorially printed items (apart from the Mulready envelope itself) to be sent through the post with their pictures visible, and set a precedent for all sorts of other innovations that were to come in later years. They were normally sold for about one shilling a dozen, and of course the postage on them was payable in addition. To satisfy a popular demand among collectors, numbers of reproductions of caricatures and other pictorial envelopes were made by a Brussels stamp dealer named M. Moens in 1868. They are easily discernible by the name F. Deraedemaeker printed on them, and have but little value.

There were several other examples of these caricatures. Some were done in the provinces, such as the very clever one published by W. H. Mason of Brighton (Mason also produced some very fine pictorially headed note-paper showing views of Brighton). Mason's envelope gives a warning against the new penny postage system, the artist (who is unknown) believing that only increased taxation would result from it. Others published by Menzies in Edinburgh, and some brought out singly by lesser known publishers, served to emphasize a particular topic of the day, at the same time lampooning Mulready's design. Many of these are extremely scarce today, but they turn up sometimes in old bookshops when least expected, and further specimens no doubt will come to light.

One of the more pleasing series to be published during 1840 was done by Fores, who engaged a young artist, only 15 years of age, at the beginning of his career. This was none other than Richard Doyle, who was later to become famous for his association with *Punch*. Young Doyle kept a diary in which he has enthusiastically commented on being given the order from Fores to do a series of six envelope designs. These were to be Courting, Musical, Dancing, Hunting, Racing and Coaching. He has recorded that his brother James was to do three of them, and it is obvious from what he has written in his diary that the brothers went to great pains in order to produce first-class results.

They were finished by September, the entry in the diary reading:

Tuesday. Glorious. Went to Fores's. The envelopes out. There they were one, two, three, four, five, six, all hung up in the window of Messrs. Fores, 41 Piccadilly, corner of Sackville Street, some of them being coloured in a very flaming and extraordinary manner. . . .

Wednesday. As sure as I am living, there was a critique on the envelopes in the "Times" this morning, and whoever dares to say there was not is a liar. Hurra!

The paragraph in *The Times* about this set of envelopes was certainly complimentary, and at the same time was able to be derogatory regarding Mulready's envelope. It reported:

FORES'S ENVELOPES

Everybody has, we presume, before this time, had an opportunity of examining those very extraordinary specimens of British Art—the penny post envelopes. On the merits of design for those absurdities we have never heard but one opinion. From Sir Robert Peel down to the lowest kitchen wench the new covers have been laughed at by every man, woman, and child of the community who has the slightest perception of the ludicrous. Anything more ridiculous could hardly be imagined, and in consequence the caricaturists have done their best to *show up* these monstrous and universally circulating libels upon the public taste. In this laudable exercise of ingenuity Mr. Fores certainly takes the lead; and we have just been favoured with a sight of a batch of envelopes published by him relating to a variety of subjects, which, in point of execution, are far superior, but which, although intended to amuse, are, we are bound to say, as regards design, far less likely to create laughter than their great prototypes. Mr. Fores's envelopes relate to hunting, courting, racing, dancing, coaching, and music, and are all excellently humorous in their respective ways. We recommend those who buy post-office envelopes merely for fun—we suppose few purchase them with any other object—to purchase Mr. Fores's envelopes instead. They are better and more amusing, both in design and execution, and are certainly more creditable to the public taste.

This set was so successful that the two brothers were commissioned to add four more to the series—Shooting,

Civic, Military and Christmas. They were finished during November, and the Christmas envelope, which was the work of Richard Doyle, can be considered the first specially printed design to commemorate Christmas, for it precedes the first Christmas card by three years.

Most prominent of all publishers of this sort of envelope was Robert W. Hume of Leith who started issuing them shortly after May 1840. Hume produced several series, comprising dozens of different designs. In a letter written by Hume and dated in May 1844, he comments how gratifying it is to have orders to the amount of hundreds of thousands of these envelopes. Yet, of the large numbers he published, comparatively few are known to collectors. In most cases, the envelope having served its purpose was thrown away; sometimes, as was the case with pictorial writing paper, the picture was cut from it and stuck into a scrap album. Their scarcity, along with their popularity among collectors today, explains the high prices they obtain in the sales-room.

Perhaps the best known of Hume's Comic Envelopes are numbers 1 to 6 in his first series. Of these, No. 2 is deserving of mention, for it sees into the future with a very humorous sketch showing Britannia carrying letters in a balloon, and alludes to a postal service to the Moon. Like most of Hume's series, the envelope was covered back and front with comic drawings, while on the flap the following instructions were given for posting letters:

Steam Letters not exceeding 100 horse power charged one penny! Eagles' feathers and bags of Rice, if pre-paid carried free!! No Coffins, except lead ones taken by Post.—Persons sending ships' masts are advised to cut them in two, waiting till receipt of the one half is acknowledged ere sending the other. Colonial letters must be marked—Balloon Letters.— Never Post your letter till the Mail has left: leaving it un-addressed also facilitates its transmission.

As well as the Comic Envelopes, Hume issued a set of Musical Envelopes pleasantly tinted in colour, showing portraits of Byron, Scott, Burns, Campbell and other poets, with their songs and music printed on the flaps. This set seems to have been combined with a series of St. Valentine envelopes (which were very crudely drawn) and numbered over seventy different designs. A small set of three called "The Tourist Envelope" was devoted to places to visit around fifty miles of Stirling, Ben Nevis and Edinburgh, and showed little views with descriptions and a map.

With this sort of pictorial envelope came a gradual transition from the caricatures poking fun at Mulready's effort, to pleasanter and more instructive designs.

It was now that the envelope was seen as a useful medium for propaganda. Already a start had been made in this respect, with the inception of uniform penny postage, by sticking on little printed labels to the fronts and backs of letters, advocating such sentiments as the Repeal of the Corn Laws, Free Trade, Temperance, and quoting Biblical verses. These little labels were sometimes used for closing up the letter. The use of the envelope now gave much

greater scope. Early examples were the two Clerical Envelopes published by A. Lesage of 21 Hanover Street, Edinburgh. These refer to the conflict between the Church and the Court of Session which preceded the disruption that took place in 1843 of the Established Church of Scotland and led to the formation of the Free Church. J. Gadsby of Manchester published two differently designed envelopes on behalf of Free Trade. The Anti-Slavery Society and various Temperance organizations used this form of publicity very freely. S. Cooper of Yeovil issued a Teetotal Letter sheet in 1843. This was tastefully ornamented with a blue border which left the space clear for the address to be written. Along one of the sides to be folded is stated:

In England and America alone, upwards of NINETY THOU-SAND DRUNKARDS are supposed to die every year; and consequently, (since, as such, dying unregenerate, they cannot be saved from the wrath to come,) they enter an awful ETERNITY, 'Where their worm dieth not, and the fire is not quenched.'

and along the other:

Drunkenness expels reason, drowns the memory, distempers the body, defaces beauty, diminishes strength, inflames the blood, causes internal, and incurable wounds, and ruins the soul! It destroys the senses, robs the purse, is the beggar's companion, the wife's woe, and the children's sorrow. It makes a

strong man weak. He is a self-murderer, who drinks to others' good health, and robs himself of his own. . . .

There were envelopes denouncing the employment of labour within the Post Office on Sunday, and a very spirited envelope known as the "Anti-Graham Envelope" was issued by *Punch* in July 1844.

It had come to the notice of the public that the letters of the Sardinian patriot Mazzini and other foreign gentlemen who had come to Britain for refuge had been opened in the Post Office and their contents revealed to foreign governments. The Home Secretary, Sir James Graham, admitted he had done this under the authority of a Queen Anne Statute, and sustained a tremendous outburst of unpopularity. *Punch* proved to be a sturdy champion of these

refugees in their plight, and for many weeks several scathing articles and cartoons against Sir James Graham's action appeared in its pages. Attempts were made to do away with the secret opening of letters, but were unsuccessful. The power to do so still remains with the Home Secretary.

The envelope that *Punch* produced caricaturing Sir James Graham was drawn by John Leech and was printed in blue. It showed Sir James in the position of Britannia with a large snake in the grass at his feet and bearing his own likeness; little nosey-parkers and busy-bodies are seen flying hither and thither, while others look through key-holes.

From propaganda it was an easy step to the use of envelopes for advertising, and because of this we have delightful examples of Victorian art in the way of shop furnishings and costume, ironmongery, the theatre and all manner of commonplace objects recorded in a manner different from the usual on the fronts, backs and insides of envelopes published during the 1850s and 1860s.

In the United States too, where the use of envelopes had come about a few years later than in Britain, advertising on

23. Valentine envelope, printed in sepia, of the American Civil war period, postmarked in 1863. (Actual size)

24. 'The Capitol, Washington.' An envelope, postmarked 1863, typical of many such as were published by Chas. Magnus. (Actual size)

26. An envelope of the American Civil War, postmarked New Orleans in 1863. (Actual size)

envelopes reached a high standard. There were views of hotels and establishments long since pulled down; old style horsedrawn carriages and street cars outside shops and warehouses covered with signs proclaiming their business; elegant footware and farm machinery of the period, all of which provides useful information to the social historian of today.

But it was during the tragic years of the American Civil War that the envelope was used so extensively for patriotic and sentimental reasons. Many hundreds of different designs, often printed in colour, were published. There were flags and shields and the American Eagle; the insignia of the Loyal States, and the badges of the Volunteer regiments; generals and popular heroes. There were comic caricatures, some for the North, and some for the South, and in these politics were prominent. There were sentimental drawings of sweethearts and wives saying farewell to their loved ones in uniform. And together with the envelopes, similarly designed note-paper was usually provided.

From all this it can be readily understood how envelopes were beginning to play an important part in the daily and social life of the people.

D

CAMP BRIGHTWOOD

Col. N. H. Davis, 7th Mass. Volunteers.

Camp Brightwood.

Washington D.C. 186/60

Lydia

I received your kind letter

27. Published in Philadelphia in 1861, with a matching envelope, of foolscap size. This sort of letter heading was much used during the American Civil War. (Actual size)

28. Heading of American Civil War note-paper, dated 1862. (Actual size)

Desperate Hand-to-Hand Encounter over a Battery.

Fort Richmond

Wednesday Oct 22nd 1862

3

PICTORIAL WRITING PAPER

OWING to a different system in rating the postage on letters, envelopes had been in use on the Continent for a great many years.[1] Examples of envelopes in a shape commonly known as such are preserved in the State archives of Geneva and date from 1615, and 18th-century specimens of French manufacture are often to be found. They were square in shape and, being unfolded, required to be closed by means of wax. According to the German encyclopaedia, Brockhaus, of 1908, the first envelopes to be made in England were produced by a stationer named Brewer in Brighton. It is believed he manufactured envelopes for the benefit of the Continental visitors, especially the ladies, and for those with the privilege of franking letters, who came to stay in the fashionable new spa of Brighthelmstone, as it was then called. English-made envelopes of a date before 1835 are very scarce, for fewer have survived than the letters they contained, and it is mainly due to the craze for autograph collecting, which was so popularly pursued in Victorian times, that the odd one can sometimes be found,

preserved because of the signature on it of the person who franked it.

By 1837, envelopes were advertised for sale in London at 2s. 6d. per dozen. Unlike 18th-century specimens, which were made by hand, these were cut and shaped by machine. They were ungummed and were required to be fastened either by gummed wafers, which were small shaped pieces of glazed paper, or by means of sealing wax.

Within a very short time of their coming into common use with the introduction of Uniform Penny Postage in January 1840, enterprising manufacturers were turning them out with tasteful decorated edges, printed in gold or silver and also in colour, often heavily ornamented with a pleasing design depicting flowers and entwined leaves or of some other decoration typifying the charm of this period.

[1] Envelopes of a sort were used in China during the middle of the Han dynasty—about the first century before Christ. Like many other inventions of the Chinese, the envelope fell into disuse and was lost for hundreds of years.

29. Headed note-paper by Rock & Co. of London. One of a series of several published in the early 1840s. (Slightly reduced)

30. One of a set of six sheets of note-paper showing domestic love, published 1840–41. (Slightly reduced)

My dear Brother

The favor of your Company is requested

My dear Wife

31, 32, 33. Examples of comic note-paper of 1841. (Slightly reduced)

34 (below). Comic note-paper heading of the 1840s reminiscent of the Railway boom. Published by Rock & Co. London. (Slightly reduced)

'Can you tell me how to make £10000 HONESTLY in Railways?'

Sometimes envelopes were embossed all over with fine cameo-type work, involving much intricacy and detail, setting a standard for which English manufacturers of this kind of work became well known.

Following the pattern set by pictorial writing paper, envelopes were published with delicately engraved little views which were often surrounded by an ornamental frame. They were usually on the fronts of envelopes, but sometimes on the flaps as well.

As a rule, envelopes and writing paper of the 1840s were rather small in size so as not to exceed the half ounce, which was the weight for the penny postage. This explains why the small pictorial writing sheets, octavo in size, now came on the market and gradually replaced the quarto size, which had been in general use over the centuries. But the quarto size remained in use for many people, particularly among the landed gentry and those who lived in stately homes, when a fine engraved view of the house would provide the heading of the writing sheet. Queen Victoria wrote her letters from Balmoral on this sort of writing paper.

With the introduction of the smaller sized note-paper, a new industry developed, and writing paper was appearing with all manner of pictorial headings suitable for all occasions. For the first time comic note-paper was published. This, sold in sets or series, usually took the form of little figures in the top left-hand corner, such as women gossiping, arguing, or quarrelling. A popular set showed well-drawn figures in comical postures, with a beginning such as: "My dear Wife", "My dear Uncle"—the dear wife shown chastising her husband, and uncle a pawnbroker. Sometimes this was varied by having a closing phrase, followed by a comic drawing in just the same way. There were sets showing children, with a beginning sentence as: "Our dear little trot looks so pretty in its new frock", or, "The sweet girl improves very much". Other sets featured dancing, riding, and other occupations. There was a set of domestic scenes showing filial, maternal, fraternal and every kind of family love, but the costume and furnishing of the background are of especial interest for the detail they depict. Topical events, such as the boom in the newly established railways, were shown, and remarkable happenings, such as the fire at the Tower of London on October 30, 1841, were recorded on note-paper within a very short time of their occurring. Costume, too, was a feature; there were series showing Welsh costume and customs, and David Hay of Edinburgh published a beautiful series illustrating the clans and their tartan, all in colour, as well as a set of Scottish fisherfolk.

By the 1850s, pictorial writing paper depicting popular scenes was available in almost every city, town and village all over the kingdom, and served exactly the same purpose as picture postcards do today. Special series were published by the famous colour printers Baxter and Le Blond, each sheet having a miniature picture printed in their patent colour process.

It was during the 1850s that several very popular series came out showing scenes at the seaside. The principal publishers of these were Newman and Co. of Watling Street, London, Rock and Co. of London and Kershaw of London. They were mostly all comical, and showed ladies in long trousered bathing dresses being scared, when in the sea, by the proximity of male bathers. Considering that men bathed in the nude at this period of our history, the alarm of the ladies is not unnatural.[1] The caption on one such sheet of paper reads: "Naiads alarmed", and, in smaller print— "It's only a little swell, Lizzy dear!" Another of the series shows the bathing machines and the very formidable "dipper", who was usually a lugubrious-looking, heavily built woman in a voluminous black costume and wearing a large bonnet, about to immerse little Franky, who is screaming his lungs out; the caption reads "There then, doesn't Master Franky like to be dipped by his Betsy? the little dove!" These women, known as dippers, were part of the seaside scene in those days. They spent hours in the water all day dipping people as soon as they emerged from their bathing machine and must have been possessed of great stamina.

[1] Caleçons, or bathing trunks, were first worn by male bathers in Brighton in 1863.

35. No. 1118 of the popular series of comic note-paper published by Kershaw & Son of London during the 1850s. (Reduced)

36. Comic seaside note-paper showing a dipper at work, published by Newman in the 1850s. (Reduced)

37 (below). Comic seaside note-paper, published by Rock & Co., 1860. (Reduced)

38. A comic American envelope showing a Polka dance in full swing. Postmarked from Virginia in the 1860s. (Actual size)

One of them, Martha Gunn of Brighton, who used to attend to the Prince Regent, was quite a celebrity for three-quarters of a century.

Other sets show families picnicking on the sands, father in his top hat and tail coat surrounded by his large family while the sea washes part of the meal away. In another picture father is shown sitting on the edge of a crowded rowing boat, the tails of his frock coat dangling in the sea. We are reminded too of the "Husbands' Boat", which was the steamer in which husbands and fathers came down from London to spend the Sunday at Ramsgate with their families, who were the "stayers". Such pictures as these, recorded in this way on writing paper, help to remind us of incidents in our social life that could so very easily become difficult to understand, or else forgotten altogether.

It was during the 1850s, too, that a great deal of propaganda was carried out by means of envelopes and note-paper. A series of events had brought to England an American philanthropist named Elihu Burritt, sometimes referred to as "the learned blacksmith".[1] This remarkable man was concerned in a movement for world peace, for universal brotherhood, and for a cheap postage across the seas. From London he organized campaigns to further these projects, and held mass meetings in all parts of the country, as well as international meetings abroad, in the cause of world peace, the first of such meetings being held in Brussels in 1848. His campaign for an Ocean Penny Postage[2] was received very seriously and was considered in high quarters by the governments of both Great Britain and the United States. Much of his publicity was carried out by means of pictorial propaganda on sets of envelopes and

39. The New Pier, Brighton, a lively scene shown on note-paper of 1868. Published by Newman & Co. of London. (Reduced)

40. Welsh costumes, depicted on note-paper of the 1850s and still popular on picture postcards of today. (Reduced)

41. "Anti-War" envelope published and used in Boston in 1852. A similar design published by J. Valentine of Dundee was used by Elihu Burritt, the American philanthropist, in his peace campaign during the 1850s. (Actual size)

writing paper. The well-known printers, Messrs. Valentine of Dundee, who were later to be one of the foremost publishers of picture postcards, published many of these propaganda envelopes in 1849.

Pictorial writing paper and envelopes were popular, not only in the British Isles but in most European countries too; but, from what has survived, it would appear that England and the United States were the two countries where the demand was greatest.

In Germany and Austria they were sold in the many holiday resorts, particularly the fashionable spas, and in Switzerland, too, delightful views showing the hotels and mountain resorts head the writing paper, as well as a beautiful series showing Swiss costume. Also, in very far distant British possessions, finely engraved headed writing paper showing the local views and sights were on sale. An interesting set showing the diggings came out at the time of the gold rush in Australia. Most of these Colonial issues were printed in London, but some of them were published locally; a fine set of harbour views was published in Valetta, Malta, early in the 1840s, and during the 1850s some beautiful sets of Australian views were published by Sands and Kenny, of Sydney and Melbourne.

In the United States, the quarto size sheets were extensively used until the 1860s when, during the Civil War, the smaller sheets printed with patriotic designs gradually superseded them.

Many of the American and Canadian pictorial letter sheets were published by Charles Magnus of New York, who produced a multitude of very fine work, much of it lithographed in colour, the illustrated headings usually covering the entire upper half of the page. An early set consisted of scenes connected with the signing of the Declaration of Independence. Others showed famous buildings, the New York firemen, Central Park and maps of towns; one delightful series of provincial cities being all in colour. Special events were commemorated as well, such as the New York Crystal Palace Exhibition of 1854, and the visit of the Prince of Wales to Canada in 1860. For these occasions the sheets were sold in large stiff envelopes which matched the size of the note-paper. With a picture on the outside, it was explained that "The Letter Sheets were for Home Correspondence, or Scrap Book Pictures".

Canadian letter-sheets for the most part were headed with excellently engraved views of the more remarkable beauty spots, Niagara Falls then, as now, being widely publicized. So also was the Victoria Bridge spanning the St. Lawrence River at Montreal, which was an outstanding feat of engineering for those days. The city of Ottawa shows as a small country town, in no way recognizable as the city it is today. The faithful reproduction of such places as they were in those days makes them especially interesting to the social historian.

It was during the 1850s and 1860s that the production of pictorial writing paper was at its peak. Every event of interest or importance was faithfully recorded by way of a

[1] So-called because as a young man he taught himself many branches of mathematics, as well as a number of foreign languages, while working at his blacksmith's anvil in Worcester, Mass.

[2] The Ocean Penny Postage movement was kept alive long after his death in 1879. It was revived in another way during the 1880s, and eventually, by the efforts of John Henniker Heaton, M.P., an Imperial Penny Postage was inaugurated on December 25, 1898.

Government House from the Botanical Gardens

42. Quarto size letter heading published in Melbourne, Australia, in 1853. (Slightly reduced)

heading. As well as the comic note-paper, there was paper printed pictorially with songs and ballads. When the Volunteer movement was started in 1852, riflemen in their green uniforms of the different towns and counties embellished the headings of the paper. With the outbreak of the Crimea War, note-paper of a patriotic design was on the market showing soldiers and sailors; one particular series was printed garishly in colour by J. T. Wood of the Strand, London, and another by W. Smith of London.

The Great Exhibition of 1851 came out in many series, also the Dublin Exhibition of 1853 and the Industrial Exhibition of 1862. All were portrayed not only on note-paper but on envelopes as well. It is recorded that the exhibit of the envelope and note-paper display at the Great Exhibition by Messrs. De La Rue and Co., the paper manufacturers, attracted a good deal of attention. Placed in the nave of the building, the newly invented envelope-folding machine was always surrounded by a crowd of interested visitors watching it turn out envelopes folded into shape and their sides

gummed, at a rate of 3,600 per hour, considered at that time to be a remarkable achievement. These envelopes carried a printed inscription on the back along the top, reading: "Machine folded and gummed by Thomas De La Rue & Co. at the Great Exhibition 1851". Others showed a coloured vignette of the Exhibition building on the flap. It was now, too, that theatres and show people advertised themselves on the fronts and backs of envelopes. An early example printed in blue on the front of an envelope and postmarked in June 1859 proclaims the appearance of "The Original and Celebrated American General Tom Thumb".

People had much more leisure in these years and, with pictorial envelopes so much in vogue, it was considered amusing to be able to write to one's friends using an envelope decorated or embellished by a design in one's own handwriting. Some of these hand-drawn efforts show real artistic merit, and, probably because of a personal association or by reason of sentiment, more seem to have survived than have the printed examples.

43. A charming letter envelope, dated from Brestenberg, Switzerland, November 1858. The two panels open as flaps, revealing the written message. (Actual size)

E*

London T.M.Inchbold 161 Fleet Str.　*N°3.*　*Engraved by John Smrdie*

The Missionary Ship TRITON leaving Bristol on her first voyage.

44. A letter heading published by Inchbold of Fleet Street, London, in the 1840s, and postmarked from Auckland, New Zealand, in August 1847. (Actual size)

The period was indeed the heyday for the little picture. By the 1840s, George Baxter perfected his colour process, so that small colour prints exquisitely produced by a cheap method were easily available for almost everyone. Everything that was portrayed was highly artistic, romantically sentimental or emotionally titillating. Baxter's patent was passed on to many licensees, and in no time the commercial possibilities of this colour process were used for the decoration of all manner of commonplace articles such as needle cases, small cardboard box lids, song titles, Sunday school reward cards, note-paper, and for all sorts of knick-knacks. Baxter tried to keep his invention a secret, but, like Gutenberg and his use of movable type, the secret could not be held for long, and others were soon printing cheaply in

colour. A result of this, early in the 1850s, was the production on a large scale of Christmas[1] and New Year cards. Conforming in size to the visiting card, they were printed in colour, with a simple message, and, thanks to the Penny Post, the public demand for them was prodigious.

Other forms of small picture cards which were on the market at this time were sets of views, finely engraved on white glazed card, similar to the engraved headings on note-paper, and sets lithographed in a pale lilac colour, sometimes gently tinted. They depicted popular seaside resorts, remarkable places of interest, beauty spots, the stately homes

[1] The first printed Christmas card, designed by John C. Horsley, R.A., was published by Henry Cole, under the name of Felix Summerly, in 1843. It was hand-coloured and showed a family party at Christmas dinner. About the size of a small postcard, only 1,000 were printed.

and castles, members of the Royal Family, and notabilities. They were sometimes available in the shape of a little book, each card joined one to the other, but easily detachable when required. Such cards were on sale in many places in the world and although some were published locally, many, especially the lithographed sets, were made in Germany, but it is noticeable how prominent were Scottish publishers with this type of work. These include such firms as Banks and Co. of Edinburgh, J. Menzies of Edinburgh (who published pictorial envelopes in the 1840s), and Nelson; in Dundee there was the old-established firm of Valentine. They were bought by visitors as souvenirs, and probably finished up in the family scrap book. No Victorian sitting room was complete without its scrap album.

Most charming of all were the "Rose" and the "Basket" sets. The "Rose" sets were manufactured in Germany and were on sale in many countries; it is probable that the "Basket" sets were also made in Germany, but this cannot be determined with certainty. A "Rose" set of views would be folded into the shape of a closed fan about three inches in length and fashioned to look like a rose on the end of a stem. When opened out it became circular, with numerous little engravings of well-known views of the locality it provided for, such as "The Rose of Edinburgh",

GUARDIANS OF ENGLAND'S HONOUR.
MARINE.

45. A letter heading printed by Kershaw & Son of London in the 1850s at the time of the Crimea War. Many series of a patriotic nature were printed by several publishers, usually in colour, during this period. (Reduced)

46. Sets of views were sold in elaborately decorated wrappers such as this. Bought as souvenirs of a place visited, the cards usually found a place in the family scrap album—circa 1850–1870. (Actual size)

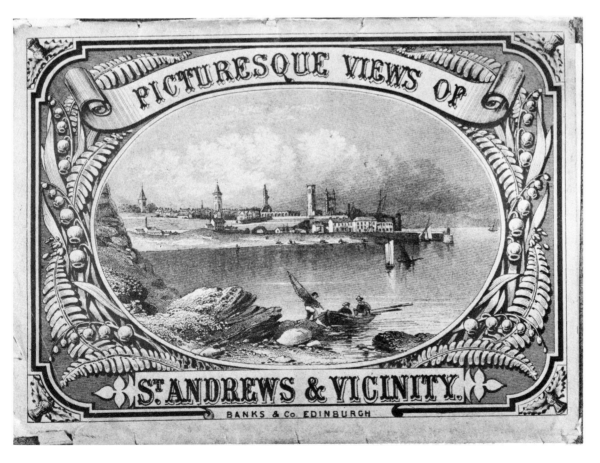

PICTURESQUE VIEWS OF
St. ANDREWS & VICINITY.
BANKS & Co. EDINBURGH

NEW YORK CRYSTAL PALACE FOR THE EXHIBITION OF THE INDUSTRY OF ALL NATIONS.

New York d. 18 Juli 1854.

47. A letter heading engraved and printed by Chas. Magnus of New York, 1853. (Slightly reduced)

48. An envelope published at the time of the Great Exhibition, 1851. (Actual size)

49. 'A London Basket.' Novelties such as this were on sale in many places both in England and abroad and were popular souvenirs. Circa 1870-1880. (Reduced)

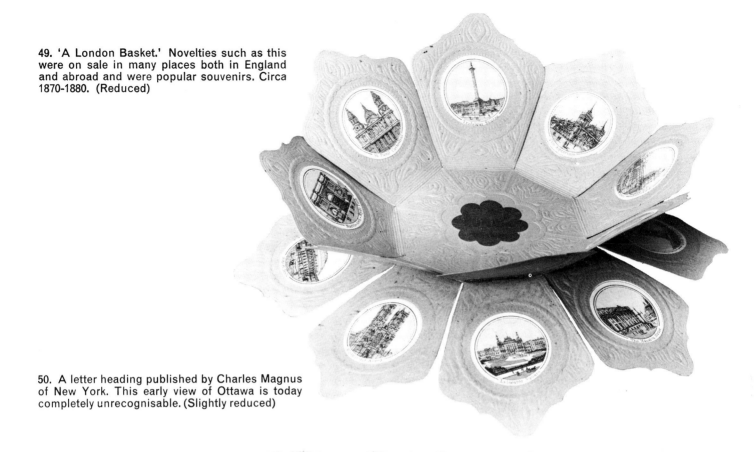

50. A letter heading published by Charles Magnus of New York. This early view of Ottawa is today completely unrecognisable. (Slightly reduced)

Published by Charles Magnus & C⁰ 12 Frankfort Street N York

OTTAWA CITY CANADA WEST.

51. H.R.H. The Prince of Wales, one of a series published by Disdéri of Paris. (Actual size)

52 (below). One of a comic series published in Berlin. (Actual size)

Angleterre, Horse Guard.

"The Rose of Cheltenham" and "The Rose of Washington", etc. The "Baskets" were similar. Made of stout brown paper, "A London Basket" would be fashioned so as to lie folded and roughly circular in shape. When opened up, it had the appearance of a water lily, with engraved views showing on all the leaves and petals.

In 1854, an event of major importance occurred when André Disdéri[1] patented the technique of producing the carte-de-visite photographs. This patent established a new size in cards, known as carte-de-visite, and Disdéri's idea was for it to take the place of the visiting card. His idea swept the civilized world, and sets of photographs carte-de-visite size came on the market everywhere. As well as personal photographs, sets of photographic pictures could be purchased in this size. These portrayed royalty, notable people, reproductions of famous works of art, views of well-known places, comic seaside scenes, costumes, stately homes and castles, and in short, everything of interest.

On the backs of these photographs were the name and address of the photographer and a word about his accomplishments. This would sometimes be followed by an announcement, as for example:

CARD, STEREOSCOPIC & CABINET, and other sizes of views of Scottish scenery sold by all the leading booksellers, and at the principal Railway book stalls in Scotland. Sets of views of Edinburgh, Trossachs, Melrose, Abbotsford, Stirling, Dunkeld, Balmoral, Staffa & Iona, Glencoe, Skye &c, in Green cloth covers for Souvenirs and Gift Books.

Most cartes-de-visite to be found today (and there are plenty available) appear to date from the 1860s, specimens of the 1850s being decidedly uncommon. The sets, judging from figures printed on them, sometimes ran into hundreds. A comic series published by J. S. and Co. of London, is numbered to 111, and there may be more. One card, from a series entitled "South Wales", showing Welsh women in costume and hand-coloured, is numbered 278. Ashford Brothers and Co. of 76 Newgate Street, London, published a great many sets of all sorts of subjects. One was a set of at least forty-eight reproductions of paintings; another example showed Queen Victoria in mourning. W. Lawrence, a well-known Dublin publisher of cartes-de-visite in the 1890s, specialized in a humorous series showing the typical comic Irishman. These were all featured again later during the 1900s when Lawrence, who was now publishing picture postcards, reproduced them in a popular series of comic Irish postcards. Cartes-de-visite were published by the principal photographers in every city and town throughout the

[1] André Adolphe Eugène Disdéri (1819-90) wrote books on photography in somewhat pompous language. "He spoke of the requirements of art, but he thought of business." From *A Hundred Years of Photography* by Lucia Moholy, Penguin Books 1939.

United Kingdom, and exactly the same sort of work was produced all over the world, as is evidenced from the numbers which are still easy to acquire.

Prices asked for a carte-de-visite size photograph varied considerably. In general, twelve cartes in London cost 21s., but in the provinces they were cheaper, 7s. 6d. for twelve being recorded as the price paid in Liverpool. For the series of views and other pictures the price was a few pence apiece, although certain special cards would cost as much as 1s. 6d. each.

The carte-de-visite became extremely popular everywhere, but although Disdéri's idea was such a success, his fame and fortune did not last and he died in poverty.

The carte-de-visite photograph did not supplant the ordinary visiting card. As already mentioned, from being a highly artistic object of beauty in the 18th century, the visiting card by the 19th century became more subdued. Sometimes the card had a satin sheen to it, or the name would be printed in an unusual, though very discreet, style of lettering. In the 1840s, in England, there was a fashion with some people for using cards decorated with an edging of paper lace-work, but this was by no means general. The tendency was for cards to be plain, so that by the middle of the century they differed very little from the engraved copper-plate card of today.

In a few Continental countries however, notably Belgium, Holland and the Rhineland, cards were still pictorially decorated. The engraving was exquisite and was often in colour. Surprisingly enough, the custom for ornamental and pictorial visiting cards lingered on in some parts of North America, particularly in the New England States, where, during the 1860s and 1870s, charming and beautiful styles, typical of the period, were still the fashion.

53. Comic carte-de-visite published by Lawrence of Dublin, one of many. All were reprinted as postcards in the 1900s. (Actual size)

54. A carte-de-visite published in colour by the Internationales Photograph: Kunst-Institut. (Actual size)

43

4

THE FIRST POSTCARD

THERE was a good deal of discussion taking place during the 1850s and 1860s for cheaper postage rates and for some form of international agreement whereby letters would be charged at a uniform rate throughout the world. In England, Elihu Burritt campaigned vigorously for an Ocean Penny Postage, and in America, Pliny Miles and Barnabas Bates worked energetically for the same movement as well as for postal reforms within the United States. Much of this campaigning was helped by means of pictorial envelopes and headed writing paper which stressed the need for postal reform and cheaper postage rates.

In 1851, on the occasion of the Great Exhibition and under the auspices of the Society of Arts, the International Postage Association was founded. Its chief aim was to secure a uniform international postage. Contacts were made with the governments of every civilized country in the world, and in October of 1852 it sent a delegate to the principal European governments to obtain more detailed information as to their opinion respecting the proposed reform. The name of the delegate entrusted to carry out this delicate mission was Manuel de Ysasi, honorary secretary of the Association. Ysasi, of Spanish origin, was a manufacturer of Toledo steel, who had settled in London in 1851.

The Association made much headway in its plans, and eventually worked out a scheme which basically was the principle eventually adopted by the General Postal Union in 1875.[1] But Ysasi never lived to see this materialize, for he came to a tragic end, losing his life at sea when the United States mail steamer *Arctic* was wrecked in September 1854. With his death the Association seems to have stagnated, for we hear little more of it. But its ideals lived on. In May 1863, through the initiative of the American Postmaster General, Montgomery Blair, a Conference was convened in Paris. This played a prominent part in the preliminary work towards the formation of a Universal Postal Union, and was the ideal aimed for by the International Postage Association, and by Manuel de Ysasi, whose name and work in this connection have been quite overlooked.

Meanwhile other postal unions had been formed, one of the most important being that of the various German states. In 1865, Dr. Heinrich von Stephan, a prominent Post Office official of the North German Confederation, was attending the Austro-German Postal Conference in Carlsruhe.[2] It was here that he explained to the other representatives of the different German States his scheme for the use of the "open post-sheet" (*offenes Postblatt*), which was the most suitable name to describe a postcard. He explained his idea in a memorial which, for the sake of its general interest and because it is so little known, in detail, is given here in its entirety:

The form of the letter, like many other human contrivances, has in the course of time undergone numerous modifications. In antiquity the wax tablets which contained the writing were united by rings; the letter was, so to speak, a book. Then came the form of the roll, which lasted until the Middle Ages. Later still, the letter assumed a more convenient form and was sent folded up, and ultimately the envelope came into use. All the principal changes were gradual and passed through various transitional stages (*Uebergangsstufen*). The material used, wax, parchment, paper, influenced the form; at one time experiments were made with thin sheets of iron as writing material. But the material alone did not decide the form of the letter, which was also modified by custom, as well as by transient fashions; by business necessities as well as by the means of conveyance adopted. From these various changes the form became ever more and more simple. This is equally true of the contents, as is shown by the extreme pomposity of the earlier epistolary style, with its formal repetition of titles, etc.

The present form of the letter does not however yet allow of sufficient simplicity and brevity for a large class of communications. It is not simple enough, because note-paper has to be selected and folded, envelopes obtained and closed, and stamps affixed. It is not brief enough, because, if a letter be written, convention necessitates something more than the bare communication. This is irksome both to the sender and the receiver. Nowadays the telegram may be said to be a kind of short letter. People sometimes telegraph in order to save the trouble of writing and sending a letter. Occasionally a visiting card is used with the same object.

These considerations suggest the need for a contrivance somewhat of the following kind, as suitable for the present time:

Let there be sold at all Post Offices, and by all postmen, forms for open communications. Let such a "post-sheet" (*Postblatt*) have the dimensions of ordinary envelopes of the larger size, and consist of stiff paper, corresponding therefore in size and quality to the recently introduced Money Orders used in some of the German Postal Districts. On the face of the card there

Sehenswürdigkeiten Berlins.

Königliche Schloss v. 10-3 Uhr tägl.	Zeughaus Mittw. Sonab. 2-4 Uhr.
Neues Museum v 10-3 U. Sontag 12-2	Waffensammlung d. Carl 10-5
Zoolog. Museum, Dienst. Freit. v 12-2	Mausoleum in Charlottenburg tgl.
Anatomisches Mus. Mittw. u Sonn 2-4	Zoologischer Garten tägl.
Mineralien Kabinet Mittw. Sonn 12-2	Gemälde Gal. d Gr Raczynski 12-2
Rauch Museum Lagerhaus tägl. 10-3	Gemälde Ausst. d Kunstvern 11-2
Schinkel Museum Bau Academie 11-1	Das Rathhaus v 9-3
Botanischer Garten täglich	Die Börse von 12-2

55. Bearing a printed message from a commercial house in Berlin, this early view card depicting famous buildings in the city was postally used in 1868. (Actual size)

might appear at the top the name of the district, and perhaps a small device (the arms of the country, etc.). On the left hand a space could be left for the date stamp of the receiving office, on the right the postage stamp already impressed upon the form. There would be a space for the address, as in Money Orders, with the printed words "To," "Office of Destination" (*Bestimmungsort*) and "Address of Addressee" (*Wohnung des Empfängers*), as well as the printed notice, "The reverse side may be used for written communications of any kind" (*Die Rückseite kann zu schriftlichen Mittheilungen jeder Art Benutzt werden*). Both the communication and the address might be written in ink, pencil, etc., but the use of the latter might detract from the clearness and permanence of the writing, especially in the address. Such a "post-sheet" would then be ready to be forwarded through the post, the postage having been paid by the purchase of the form. The charge for postage should be fixed as low as possible, say about 1 silver groschen, irrespective of the distance the form is conveyed. Apart from the postage, no charge should be made for the form itself.

As already proved in the case of Money Orders, the manipulation of the "post-sheets" in the technical Postal Service would present no difficulty, on account of their uniform shape, their clear manner of address, and their being ready stamped.

To the public the arrangement would be welcome on many occasions and for many purposes, especially when the first

aversion to open communications had been overcome by a closer consideration of the matter. How very troublesome, for instance, it is at present for anyone on a journey who wishes to write to his relatives telling them of his safe arrival or asking for some article that may have been forgotten! In the future such a one would take a 'post-sheet' from his portfolio, and with a lead pencil, in the carriage or on the platform, fill it up and post it in the nearest pillar-box or railway letter box. It is probable that in addition to its use for social purposes a large number of orders, advices &c., in connection with business transactions, would be forwarded *per Postblatt*.

The idea received the fullest consideration but was ultimately rejected because it was thought that the German postal administration, composed as it was of so many different States, lacked the necessary uniform administration to carry it out, and, moreover, it was believed that it might result in a loss of revenue.

Although officially the idea was not taken up, it is known that cards were produced privately and some used within

[1] In 1878 this became the Universal Postal Union.

[2] In April 1870 Von Stephan became General Post Director of the North German Confederation, and in 1876, Postmaster General of the Imperial German Empire.

56. A card celebrating the 25th Jubilee of the introduction of the postcard by Austria. Issued in Vienna, January 26, 1894, honouring Dr. Emanuel Herrmann. (Reduced)

the North German Confederation. Business houses used cards bearing a printed notice on one side to announce the visit of their representatives or to draw attention to market prices or other business easily and quickly explained in a short message. A card of this sort in the author's collection is from a manufacturer in Berlin. The top half gives the name of the firm in Berlin and announces that their representative will be calling within a few days' time. The lower half is taken up by the name and address, alongside which a postage stamp of the North German Confederation is affixed and cancelled with the date: 22.11.68. The other side of the card is embellished with several attractive little views and is captioned *Sehenswürdigkeiten Berlins* (places of interest to be seen in Berlin), the places being listed with their times for visiting. In size the card measures 7 by 4½ inches. It is indeed a very early example of a pictorial card, postally used.

In France, too, business houses used plain cards, of usual size, for the purpose of sending short announcements or by way of an invoice. Such cards were rated one centime postage, the rate for printed matter. Reference is sometimes made to an early pictorial card posted in Basle in 1865, which was shown at the International Exhibition of Postcards in Paris in 1900. In Germany during the 1860s, pictorial cards were sent as invitations to hunts, and it is known also that in England during the 1860s people sometimes posted their visiting cards, bearing a short message and franked with a 1d. stamp. A firm of colour manufacturers in Leith named Lundy was in the habit of using small cards of normal envelope size, bearing short printed business messages, between 1860 and 1870,[1] and between 1850 and 1860 it is related how Nicholas Parry, Master of the Puckeridge Hounds, used to send a home-made card by the

post every week, to advise of hunt meets.[2] In the absence of a postcard rate, the postage on these cards in England was rated the one penny or Book Post rate. But earliest of any card under the true name of a postcard is that of Lipman in Philadelphia. Inscribed "Lipman's Postal Card", a patent was entered and applied for in Philadelphia in 1861. Only four of these early cards are known, and all are in unused condition (see Appendix I).

A few years after Dr. von Stephan's proposal, a young Austrian professor of economics, Dr. Emanuel Herrmann of Vienna, wrote an article in the *Neue Freie Presse* proposing the use of postcards, pointing out how the importance of the contents of large numbers of letters sent by post was out of all proportion to the time and trouble taken in writing them, for the sake of the few polite sentences involved. Such letters, he suggested, could as well be sent on an open card, and for less postage (see Appendix II).

His arguments so impressed the Austrian Post Office that they forthwith carried them into operation, and on October 1, 1869, the world's first postcard came into being.

Whether or not Dr. Herrmann had any knowledge of Dr. von Stephan's original proposal for just such a postcard will never be determined. However, the facts are that the new Austrian postcard which was produced by the Austrian Postal Administration conformed to a prescribed size and was entirely in accordance with the plan suggested by Dr. von Stephan. The cards were thin and buff coloured. Arched above a small device of the Austrian emblem was printed *Correspondenz-Karte*, while in the top right-hand corner

Rudelsburg.

57. An early viewcard dated 1874, in Mrs. Marion Moriarty's collection. This won the Silver Medal at the International Exhibition in Nice, 1899. (Reduced)

was imprinted a yellow 2 kreuzer stamp. Three lines were ruled for the address, and the message was to be written on the other side. Dr. Herrmann's claim as inventor of the postcard was soundly contested by the German postal authorities, but the claim was supported by his own country, and the world will always recognize Austria as having produced the first postcard. In any case, Dr. Emanuel Herrmann was certainly responsible for this happening.

In no time the postcard proved its popularity and usefulness, which is more than shown by the 2,926,102 cards sold in Austria-Hungary during their first three months of sale.

This unqualified success induced other countries to follow suit. The North German Confederation was the next to issue postcards, on July 1, 1870, the price being fixed at one silver groschen, which was the charge for ordinary inland letters, therefore to the public using them there was no benefit of a reduced postage. On the first day 45,468 cards were sold in Berlin alone. The scheme was gradually adopted by all the South German States as well, and soon was taken up all over Germany, after which an agreement was entered into within their postal system; this Union was then joined by Austria-Hungary in August of 1870.

Next to issue postcards, together with Switzerland, was the United Kingdom, on October 1, 1870. On this day, too, the first halfpenny postage stamp was issued. The idea of postcards in Britain was first brought to the notice of the Government, and to the public, in an article which appeared in the *Scotsman* of September 17, 1869, but several other individuals had proposed their use as well. Nothing came of the idea, and it was not until February 17, 1870, that Dr. Lyon Playfair[3] presented to the Government a lengthy memorial containing many signatures in favour of a "*card post*".

The Government was now in a better position to consider the proposal and was able to enquire of the Austrian Postal Administration as to the success of the postcard in that country. As a result of this, on May 26, 1870, the Postmaster General recommended to the Treasury the use of postcards. The official machinery was then set in motion, and as already stated, postcards were placed on sale on the first of October (see Appendix III).

It is perhaps strange to understand, however, that some

58. An early form of view card used in Germany. View of the Schneekoppe, postmarked July 22, 1873. Reproduced by courtesy of Mirko Verner. (Reduced)

sections of the public were strongly opposed to the use of postcards. They imagined that it would become all too easy for people to read other people's messages and private concerns, and that it would become easy for people to indulge in public libel and defamation of character as a means of venting their spite and malice. There were others, too, who considered the use of a halfpenny postcard to be an insult, believing that if a penny was not paid for a message, then it was hardly worth sending at all; for many years the use of postcards was frowned upon by a certain class of person. However, they were good enough for Mr. Gladstone, who was accustomed to write much of his large correspondence with the aid of the halfpenny postcard. Curiously enough, among the more responsible and important people to raise objections was the Society of Arts—the same who had so ardently supported the International Postage Association. This Society suggested the use of a blue light-weight letter-sheet, to be folded into the shape of an envelope, not unlike the modern air letter of today, though somewhat smaller. For the purpose of propaganda, the Society published an envelope of this sort which carried several proposals printed in very small lettering. Inside, underneath the flap, was printed "Writing to be inside this Envelope so as to discourage the curiosity of 'Paul Prys' ".

This was followed by :

"QUESTION,—If the Post Office is able to supply a card, stamp it, carry it, and deliver it to any part of the United Kingdom,—why cannot the Post Office stamp an Envelope weighing less than the card and supplied by the public, thus saving the cost of the card, and discouraging impertinent curiosity, and deliver it like a letter? Every Member of Parliament who understands administrative economy is advised to ask the Postmaster General this question in Parliament until it is satisfactorily answered."

[1] An example of one of Lundy's cards is in the Post Office archives in London.

[2] From *Titbits*, in whose columns appeared in June 1889 a correspondence, "Who was the inventor of the Postcard?"

[3] Dr. Lyon Playfair devoted his whole life to public affairs and was interested in all aspects of social welfare. He was a Member of Parliament and later became Postmaster General for a short period under Gladstone (1873). In 1892 he was made Baron Playfair of St. Andrews. He died in 1898.

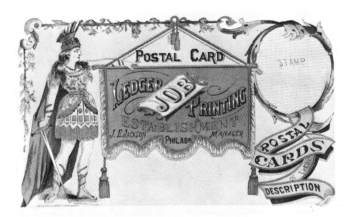

59. An advertisement postcard of a Philadelphia printer, 1873. Published in full colour. Reproduced by courtesy of Mr. Norman Shepherd. (Reduced)

On the outside of the flap was:

"Specimen Envelope, issued by the Society of Arts, weighing about 2 grains less than a Postcard."

On the address side was printed along the top:

"Specimen of an Envelope of which the paper is to be found by free trade and sent to be stamped, or stamped by an adhesive stamp, which it is proposed by the *Society of Arts* should be substituted for the Post Card produced by Government monopoly and unnecessary interference with trade."

The Royal Arms were featured in the centre, with a squared blank printed for a halfpenny postage stamp to be affixed.

Notwithstanding all the objections raised against them, the demand for the new postcards was very great. On the first day of sale 575,000 cards were dealt with at the General Post Office alone, while throughout the country nearly 1,500,000 were posted weekly during the first few weeks. In their first year of use, the number of cards posted was 75 millions! There can be no doubt as to their popularity and usefulness, and many people kept their first postcards postmarked on the day of issue as a souvenir, which is very fortunate for collectors today, for such cards are not uncommon.

They were made in two sizes on thin buff card, approximately 4¾ by 3½ inches and 4¾ by 3. Printed in lilac along the top were the words POST CARD above the Royal Arms, under which was the instruction: THE ADDRESS ONLY TO BE WRITTEN ON THIS SIDE. In the right-hand top corner was imprinted the Queen's Head, and a neat frame surrounded the whole. The back of the card was for the message. The cards were sold for 6d. a dozen, and this gave rise to much discontent among stationers and paper manufacturers who protested that the Post Office was creating a

monopoly by including the card with the price of the halfpenny postage. Eventually, after much discussion with manufacturers and other interested people, a settlement was reached in 1872 when it was decided to charge 6½d. for a dozen cards, and private cards, which hitherto had not been allowed, could be used if sent to Somerset House[1] to be imprinted with the Queen's Head postage stamp. The printing of private cards started on June 17, 1872, and was greatly appreciated by the public in general, especially by those in business. In June 1874 senders were allowed to write their signatures on the address side of postcards, and on February 1, 1875, a thicker quality card was on sale at 8d. per dozen, the thinner cards going up in price to 7d. a dozen. But for many years to come the use of the postcard was restricted by rules. It was because of the regulations governing them that picture postcards—already being used in some countries—were not permitted to be published at this time in Britain, and it was to require a good deal of arguing and hammering against Post Office officialdom before postcards were freed from some of those regulations.

Because of the colossal amount of extra business brought about by the use of postcards, the Post Office found itself unable to cope with the cancelling of so many, for the number of cancelling machines was quite inadequate for the enormous number of cards being used. Quite often, postcards went through uncancelled, which made it necessary for a new Post Office instruction that henceforth, as from October 1870, the use of cut-out imprinted stamps stuck on letters in lieu of postage stamps was no longer allowed.[2]

From the latter part of 1870 until some time during 1873 machines were used which, instead of cancelling, punched

60. A pictorial advertisement as published on the first day of issue of the halfpenny postcard, 1st October, 1870. (Reduced)

61. This design was one of a series which was printed on the first English halfpenny postcard for Christmas 1870. It is the earliest known postcard printed in colour and was published by John S. Day of Savoy Street, Strand, London. (Actual size)

holes in the place where the imprinted stamp was, or notched the card at the side, in much the same way as a ticket collector's punch. Many people raised objections to this form of cancelling, as sometimes the message on the back of the card became mutilated. After 1873 these machines, which had been used in London, Liverpool and Manchester, were taken out of service.

By now many countries had adopted the postcard system. Belgium and Holland introduced it on January 1, 1871, and three months later, on April 1, postcards were on sale in Denmark, Norway and Sweden. Canada was the first country in the Empire to introduce postcards early in 1871. Russia followed suit on January 1, 1872, and France on January 13, 1873. The United States considered the idea in 1870 but delayed until May 1873 before eventually issuing them; but, when they did, the demand was prodigious and no less than 60 million cards were sold during the first six months (see Appendix V). That same year Serbia, Romania, Spain and Italy all issued postcards.

With the creation of the postcard a new era in our social life was begun in which the postcard was to prove its usefulness in a great variety of ways, apart from changing the writing habits of many people. Brevity was essential to enable people to write as much as possible in the small space provided. Long descriptive phrases and lengthy expressions of endearment which were so commonly used in letter writing now gave place to a minimum number of words.

[1] See Appendix IV. Postage stamps as well as Revenue stamps were sometimes printed at Somerset House.

[2] This remained in force until January 1, 1905, and since that date the use of printed stamps cut from postcards or Post Office envelopes is allowed.

As was the case in Britain, some countries imposed rules and regulations which limited the use of postcards; these mainly concerned the size, the method of address, and the prohibition of anything except a brief message in the space provided. In the early years of their use it was not permitted for postcards to be sent out of the country, and in Britain, when this happened, such cards would be marked in red with a framed two-lined stamp reading "NOT TRANSMISSIBLE TO PLACES ABROAD" and returned to the sender. In the U.S.A. it was permitted for postal cards to be sent to certain listed European countries at a 2 cents rate.

In some countries, notably Germany, Austria and Switzerland, there were fewer restrictions, and it was not long after their introduction that postcards were on sale in Germany with small views of resorts and interesting places printed on them; frequently a hotel or restaurant would be depicted. These were very simply printed in black or brown as a heading or sometimes along the edge on cards imprinted with the current 5 pfennige postage. Similar cards were used in Austria, where, early in the 1880s, New Year greetings were printed on them.

An early pictorial card is reported from France, where, at the time of the Franco-Prussian war in 1870, one Leon Bésnardeau, a bookseller of Sillé-le-Guillaume in the district of Sarthe, designed, printed and sold cards having a patriotic motif to the soldiers and sailors encamped at Conlie, near Le Mans. To date, no original of this card has come to light, and it is known only because reproductions were made of it in about 1903 from the original plate.

The Prussians, too, issued Field Post Cards in 1870 for the use of their troops, and a series is known with humorous designs bearing somewhat suggestive verses.

F

Another card used in this war is of particular interest for being not only an early postcard, but also an early airmail. When Paris was besieged by the Prussians, small lightweight cards weighing only three grammes were specially issued by a decree of September 25, 1870, and were prepared for use for despatch by balloon. This was not a government venture but a private initiative. At first, the cards were inscribed by the hand of the sender "Par Ballon Monté", then, from the beginning of October 1870, they were printed with the inscription PAR BALLON NON MONTÉ, or PAR BALLON LIBRE, in two lines. The cards bore a simple centre ornament of a cluster of tricolours, with adequate space left for the address, and a place to affix a 10 centimes postage stamp.

In spite of a few mishaps, the experiment on the whole was successful and some sixty-five ascents were made, of which only fifty-six carried mail. It is extraordinary that the French Post Office having this practical proof of the usefulness of the postcard delayed until January 1873 before issuing them to the public.

Next after Austria to issue postcards was the North German Confederation on June 1, 1870. At first called *Korrespondenzkarte*, the name was changed to *Postkarte* on March 1, 1872. Within a short time of their appearance a bookseller and printer of Oldenburg named A. Schwartz printed on them, in the opposite corner to the postage stamp, a little figure of a soldier and a cannon. So far, only one example of this card is known. Postmarked July 16, 1870, it is considered by many to be the world's earliest

pictorial postcard, printed as it is on a government-issued card.

Until July 1, 1872, the German Post Office did not permit postcards to be issued by private enterprise, so that pictorial cards could only be printed on the government-issued postcards, which explains why none is known, with the exception of the one printed by Schwartz. When this restriction was removed, in 1872, publishers at once issued greetings and New Year cards in the form of postcards to be sent through the post. The year 1872 probably marks the date of the first German pictorial cards. It was during this year that a Zurich publisher, J. H. Locher, issued a set of Zurich views, made in Nuremberg—considered the earliest known views to be printed on postcards. Very soon cards, headed with views of well-known places, and always uncoloured, were published in many German cities and towns; favourites among these were those showing a picture of a castle. The idea of pictures and views on postcards was then taken up by hotels and restaurants, for although the same sort of views for years past had been shown on writing paper, their advertising potential was now becoming much more effective.

Schwartz was very likely responsible for the cards printed with the little view of the Schneekoppe in the Riesengebirge; known copies of this rare card are postmarked in July 1873. Probably other views of this sort were printed which still remain to be discovered. A set of twenty-five illustrated cards was also published by Schwartz in 1875.

Britain's first pictorial cards were prepared a little ahead of time so as to be posted on the first day of issue—October 1, 1870. Although pictorially printed on the Post Office halfpenny cards, they were of course quite unofficial, and in the nature of advertisements. A notable example was the one issued by the Royal Polytechnic Institute of Regent Street, London, which announced a programme of entertainment with a message which "welcomes the introduction of the Half-Penny Postage, by Presenting one of its first Issues to its Numerous Patrons". To enable cards to be suitably printed ahead of time for the first day of the halfpenny postage, the Post Office supplied sheets of forty-two cards in minimum numbers of 240 sheets at a cost of £21 payable in advance.

Christmas greetings, lithographed in colour, and printed on the backs of the Post Office halfpenny postcards, were published by John S. Day of Savoy Street, Strand, London, in 1870, and soon after the first government postal cards came out in the U.S.A. in 1873, American greetings cards manufacturers were quick in publishing Christmas and New Year cards on the backs of them.

An early pioneer pictorial card was the inspiration of Petar Manojlovic's, a young Serbian officer, who designed it while in Vienna engaged in his military service. Engraved by R. von Waldheim of Vienna, this card was decidedly of Balkan interest, obviously intended for the benefit of the Serbian population residing at that time in Vienna. Very prominently featured was a dragon which in Serbian language is called *Zmaj*, but was also the name of a Serbian

63. A unique card printed and posted in Vienna in May 1871. One of the earliest known picture postcards. Reproduced by courtesy of Mirko Verner. (Reduced)

newspaper published in Vienna at that time. Petar Manojlovic, who was a friend of the editor of this paper, gave the design to him, and the paper subsequently issued it as a pictorial card.

Patriotic note-paper printed in colour was published in France at the time of the Franco-Prussian War, and in the United States the American Peace Society of Boston issued a set of envelopes stressing the need for world peace.

A set of anti-clerical envelopes, comically drawn, came out about now in France. Printed in black on buff envelopes, they were very virulent in their propaganda, proclaiming on the flaps:

64. An envelope of patriotic design printed in colour and published by J. C. Wilson of Montreal. Postcards of similar design were also published. (Actual size)

SOLDIERS OF THE QUEEN.
"Where's the Coward that would not dare
To fight for such a Queen".

65. Headed writing paper, published by Chas. Magnus of New York in 1850s. (Slightly reduced)

Les Prêtres ne sont pas que le Peuple pense;
Notre credulité fait toute leur science. (Voltaire)
Le Cléricalisme, voila l'Ennemi! (Gambetta)
L'existence d'une corporation clericale quelconque est incompatible avec la liberté. (Louis Blanc)
Écrasons l'Infâme! (Voltaire)

These were sold in Paris at the shop of Mme Marie Taxil, who styled herself Directrice of the Anti-clerical Library, 35 Rue des Écoles. They cost 1 fr. 25 for one hundred assorted comic envelopes, which, it was stated, were allowed to be sold!

During the 1880s an amusing set of political envelopes caricaturing Mr. Gladstone came out in England and enjoyed some measure of popularity. But the era of the pictorial envelope was nearly over. At Christmas time a few prettily designed envelopes came on the market, and were mainly for children. There were a few sets of envelopes drawn in black and white showing coaching and country scenes of a light humour. Nothing that was now being produced in any way compared with the charming designs of the 1850s and 1860s.

One of the last of the envelope designers of any note was Alfred Gray. He became well known for his greetings cards which, drawn in black and white, were of a style far in advance of their time. He was an exponent also of the "aesthetic" craze and produced several amusing and clever drawings in this vogue. His envelopes and note-paper were always comical, but well drawn and typical of the late Victorian era.

So, with pictorial envelopes and writing paper about to go out of fashion, pictorial postcards were now coming in. They marked the beginning of what was to become a gigantic industry, and were responsible for one of the biggest collecting crazes the world has ever known.

52

5

THE FIRST PICTURE POSTCARDS

An event of major importance happened in 1874 when a General Postal Union was created in Bern, Switzerland. The outbreak of the Franco-Prussian war had prevented further meetings and discussions taking place, and it was largely due to the painstaking efforts of the German postal reformer, Dr. Heinrich von Stephan, who, after the formation of a unified Germany became that country's Postmaster General, that the first Congress and International Postal Treaty[1] was successfully brought about and took effect from July 1, 1875.

One very important agreement reached at the Congress was the fixing of a unit rate of 25 centimes (2½d.) postage rate for letters sent to all member countries of the Union. For the first time postcards were discussed on an international level, and it was agreed for postcards to be sent abroad between member countries at half the letter rate, i.e. for one penny-farthing. Thereupon a new postcard was issued by Great Britain, printed in brown on buff, and headed in two lines: "FOREIGN POST CARD. For Countries included in the Postal Union". Today we give no thought when we send a postcard to a country overseas; such a common everyday action is assumed by many to have always been possible. Few people realize that it required

days and hours of discussion at an international meeting attended by the top postal officials of the civilized countries of the world in order to come to an agreement to do this. As a boon to business this penny-farthing card was invaluable, and the saving in postage to business houses with large overseas connections was incalculable.

This penny-farthing postcard came so near to being the answer to the efforts of the many who had campaigned over the years for an international penny rate; yet it was soon forgotten and had only a short life, for in 1879 new overseas rates were introduced (see Appendix VI).

On January 1, 1878, the design of the domestic halfpenny postcard was altered a little and the colour changed to brown. It was probably during this year that attempts were made to undercut the Post Office by advertising contractors who offered postcards to the public at a cost of 2s. 6d. per 100. The message side of these postcards was covered on all four edges with numerous small advertisements placed within panels, space being left in the centre for the written message. They were printed by The Farthing Letter Card

[1] At the second Congress held in Paris in 1878 the name was changed to Universal Postal Union.

66. Advertisements allowed these halfpenny stamped postcards to be sold for 2s. 6d. per 100. (Actual size)

F*

Company Ltd., of 11 Queen Victoria Street, London. Another sort, called "The Churchman's ¼d. Post Card", was published by the Church Agency of 31 Threadneedle Street, London; possibly there were others. This was merely the adoption of the same idea which was tried in 1840 when the Mulready letter-sheets were sold at less than cost, made possible by having the inside of the sheets covered with small advertisements. Cut rate cards were also published in the U.S.A. as well as in certain European countries; some were allowed by government sanction.

Abroad, a few countries, notably Switzerland and Austria as well as Germany, were publishing postcards in the 1880s, printed in one colour, but usually in black with little views on them. These sometimes headed the card, or would be shown along the side, or in one corner. A year or two later Switzerland was producing coloured cards showing a picture or view nearly all over, but with sufficient space left blank for a short message to be written. These early Swiss cards have a decided charm about them, all their own. One sort in particular, which turns up frequently, shows the famous Rigi Kulm Hotel, on top of the Rigi, on Lake Lucerne (demolished only recently to make way for a modern hotel). There are many different views of this; some show the little mountain train (the oldest mountain railway in the world), others show groups of tourists admiring the view, with the hotel in the background looking like a huge gothic mansion perched on high. Somewhere in the picture is often a bunch of edelweiss or alpine rose. Other delightful examples show Swiss costumes, while some are devoted to alpine scenes.

The Swiss were among the earliest in the field with coloured picture postcards, much of the printing being done in Zurich and Wintherthur.

When the Paris Exhibition was held in 1889, a popular souvenir was the postcard sold at the Eiffel Tower, the main attraction of the exhibition. There was more than one design, but all showed a picture of the famous tower, with space for the message to be written.

As was the case in the 1850s and 1860s, when pictorial envelopes and note-paper were issued appropriately printed for the exhibitions of those years, postcards were now published for many of the exhibitions being held all over Europe.

In London, an officially printed card was issued on the occasion of the celebration of the Jubilee of Penny Postage, when, from May 16 to May 19, 1890, an exhibition of postal history interest was held at historic Guildhall. This was a buff card of normal present-day size, printed in red. The arms of the City of London featured in the centre, while an ornamental device of the royal monogram V.R. showed in the top left corner, and the penny postage stamp was printed in the top right.

It is interesting to consider why a penny was charged for postage instead of the usual ½d. postcard rate. Technically it was not a postcard but a commemoration card. At this time an inland postcard could not exceed the then normal ½d. size, hence the Guildhall card bears a penny postage stamp, representing the letter rate, and not the postcard rate. Only 10,000 were printed. They were quickly sold at 6d. each,

Du bist ein Freund von schönen
Mädchen,
Liebst auch so manche Kellnerin,
Drum send ich Dir anbei
dies Bildchen,
Es ist gewiß nach
Deinem Sinn.

67. An early comic card of the 1880s, printed in two colours. (Actual size)

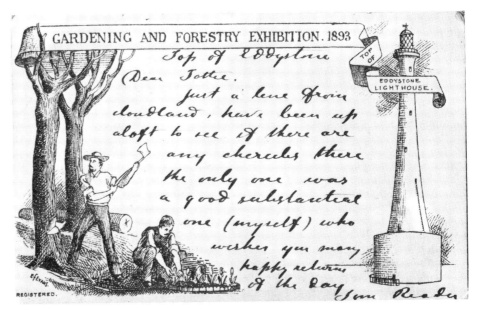

68. A rare card issued for the Gardening and Forestry Exhibition of 1893, printed in blue. (Actual size)

for the benefit of the Rowland Hill Benevolent Fund. They represent an early attempt made by the British Post Office to commemorate an event and are the forerunners of all the special commemorative postage stamps which are now issued so frequently. A special date stamp of ornamental design was used for cancelling them which proved to be very popular. At the time it was rumoured that the card with its special postmark would soon be very valuable, consequently the entire issue was sold out within three hours!

A few months later, on July 2, 1890, another exhibition took place at the South Kensington Museum celebrating the same event. This time a special pictorial envelope printed in blue was issued depicting the postal progress made in the fifty years between 1840 and 1890. Inside the envelope was a correspondence card, having a picture of Rowland Hill, and an ornamental heading inscribed "He gave us Penny Postage". This envelope and card sold for one shilling, the proceeds also going to the Rowland Hill Benevolent Fund. About 148,000 were sold, which explains why they are fairly easy to come by today. Although the correspondence card was intended only for a message enclosed within the envelope, many people used it as a postcard, in spite of the fact that it in no way conformed to the rules and regulations for postcards at that time. Some people, believing maybe that Rowland Hill's portrait was in lieu of a postage stamp, posted them without sticking on a stamp. Others affixed a halfpenny or a penny stamp. These early pictorial cards postally used in this way are scarce and desirable.

A clever caricature of this envelope and card was drawn by the well-known artist Harry Furniss. The drawings called attention to the lot of the hard-working British postman with his low pay for long hours. These, when found in postally used condition, are very scarce indeed.

In 1891 a postcard was issued in connection with the Royal Naval Exhibition held at Chelsea Hospital, when a model of Eddystone Lighthouse was built in the grounds. To the left of the message side of the card was printed a sketch of this with the caption "Top of the Eddystone Lighthouse". In a small Post Office at the top of the model, special post cards having a picture of the lighthouse were sold at 1s. each, the proceeds going to naval charities. A large commemorative handstamp, ornamental in design, was used to cancel the cards which were posted there.

Another similarly designed card is known bearing the inscription "INTERNATIONAL EXHIBITION 'OLD AMERICA' MANCHESTER", but information as to its use and date is uncertain, as no such exhibition is recorded as having taken place in Manchester.

The idea of the lighthouse must have been popular, for

69. Special postmarks used at the Royal Naval Exhibition, London, 1891, and the Gardening and Forestry Exhibition, Earl's Court, 1893. These are much sought after by collectors today. (Actual size)

55

70. An early "Gruss aus" card dated 1891, printed in one colour —brown. (Reduced)

71. A "Gruss aus", published for Schaffhausen, Switzerland, 1897. (Reduced)

72. "Souvenir de Roubaix", posted in 1898. This style of pictorial card, usually printed in Germany, was sold throughout the world. (Reduced)

the same model was erected again at Earls Court in 1893 on the occasion of the Gardening and Forestry Exhibition. Again a small Post Office was installed at the top of the lighthouse where special picture postcards printed in blue were sold and cancelled with a large decorative cancellation. These pictorial postcards of the 1890s are the earliest to have been used in Great Britain, and in postally used condition are of considerable rarity.

Whereas by this time—the 1890s—pictorial view cards were widely sold in many European countries, no such cards were available in Britain or the U.S.A., where the post office regulations were as severe as those in Britain and prevented the issue of privately printed picture postcards, probably to protect the sales of their own Post Office cards, although these too were somewhat late on the market, coming out as they did in 1873.[1] It was also due to the confusing regulations concerning postal rates, that private manufacturers were discouraged from publishing picture postcards, although a few made the attempt, notably the American Souvenir Company of Boston. This firm published pictorial cards similar to the European *Gruss Aus* designs, bearing a copyright dated 1895. The firms of Kreh, and Livingston in New York were publishing in 1897, as well as Schaefer in Philadelphia; and there were others too in different parts of the States. Such cards, dated before 1898, are scarce to find.

In Germany, Austria and Switzerland extremely beautiful cards showing three or four views of places of interest to see or visit in a town or resort were now being produced. Amidst an elaborate ornamental framework and clusters of flowers, the words "Gruss Aus" (Greetings From) were printed, followed by the name of the place, adequate space being left for the message or greeting. At first, about the year 1890, such cards were printed in one colour only, but fairly clear-cut and often glossy, sometimes in a dark brown tone or in blue-brown; the next step was for them to be printed in two colours, usually brown and blue.

The removal of the many restrictions that applied to postcards in Britain had been pressed for on several occasions in the House of Commons by Mr. John Henniker Heaton, the Member for Canterbury. Ever since his election to Parliament, in 1886, Mr. Henniker Heaton had championed many different types of postal reform and was a constant embarrassment to the Postmaster General. Among his many questions referring to postcards was the one concerning their cost to the public. Following the deputation

[1] Pictorial trade cards and other advertisements of a postcard size were sometimes sent through the post during the 1870s and 1880s. These sometimes depicted views and places of historic interest. Worthy of note are the Exhibition advertisement postcards of 1873 (Chicago) and 1874 (Cincinnati) which were printed, uncoloured, on the first government postal cards of 1873.

of paper and card manufacturers to the Postmaster General in 1870, when they protested against the card being included with the halfpenny postage, a slight rise in price to the public resulted, to be followed by another small increase in 1875. Not long after his election to Parliament in 1886, Mr. Henniker Heaton protested that the General Post Office was making a profit out of the cards beyond the value of the halfpenny postage, at the expense of the public. In 1890, while debating the cost of a million postcards and a million halfpenny stamps, he argued that it might well be cheaper to allow people to affix postage stamps to their postcards than to compel them to buy postcards supplied to the Post Office by the Government contractors (Messrs. De La Rue). This suggestion was firmly turned down because the Post Office was making a handsome profit out of the sale of cards. But Henniker Heaton was not to be quietened and he persisted in his proposals for an issue of plain postcards without the imprint of the postage stamp for the public to use by affixing their own postage stamps.

Persistent agitation finally produced the desired result, and on September 1, 1894, the General Post Office allowed privately printed postcards of a specified size (see Appendix VIII). This opened the door to private enterprise, and picture postcards generally known as such, and distinct from the pictorial advertisements which had appeared on them from their inception in 1870, were now able to be published and sold throughout the British Isles.

The new postcards were not without restriction and their maximum size had to correspond as nearly as possible to the size of the ordinary postcard then in use. The next year a slight change was made, by the introduction of the "court" or correspondence card. The court cards were 4½ ins. by 3½ ins., and the views that came to be printed on them had necessarily to be very small. Two or three little vignettes, entwined together by decorative framework, were usually printed in one of the corners, the rest of the card being left blank for the message. The derivation of the word "court" as applied to postcards is somewhat obscure, although a few fanciful theories have been suggested, the popular one being that Queen Victoria favoured this size, and that they were used by the court. The *Shorter Oxford English Dictionary* explains a court card to be of or belonging to a royal court, and that it is a variation of a coat-card, i.e. a court card in a pack of playing cards. This might be a possible meaning, and it is interesting to remember how playing cards, in the very beginning established a size for visiting cards, when they first came into general use. But very likely where postcards are concerned, the word derives from the French word *court* meaning short. In contradiction to this however, the Post Office description on packet wrappers is "COURT-SHAPE STOUT POST CARDS", which emphasizes the shape of the card and not its size.

By 1895 the "Gruss Aus" cards of German manufacture, appropriately inscribed for use in many countries, were becoming increasingly popular, and by the end of the century they were on sale almost all over the world. Whoever had thought of the simple idea of printing "Greetings From" on a prettily designed picture postcard little knew

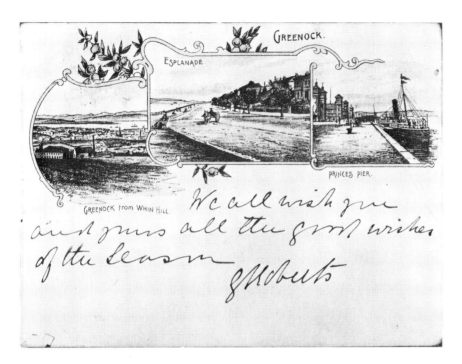

74. A typical viewcard, published by Valentine of Dundee and used in 1899. (Actual size)

to what extent he would revolutionize the entire postcard industry.

Until now the public had been somewhat indifferent to the use of picture postcards printed simply in one colour. In England they were scarcely known, and only the advertiser saw the possibilities in a pictorial postcard. But now people could send an artistically printed souvenir in the form of a picture postcard brightly coloured, and showing the exciting and interesting place they were writing from, especially from places abroad and far away. For at this time, during the 1890s, foreign travel, although mainly for the more privileged classes, was already within the reach of the more venturesome person of moderate means. The pioneer travel company of Thos. Cook and Son had facilities for the ordinary person to enjoy a continental holiday anywhere, at reasonable prices, and had organized tours to Egypt and the Middle East on a scale never before achieved. The Polytechnic Touring Association of London had established themselves on the lakeside near Lucerne, and Dr. Henry Lunn was busy organizing travel for clergymen and their families in Switzerland. In the 1890s, Bennett's Travel Agency issued picture postcards boosting their Scandinavian tours, and Cook's had postcards with their name on, available at the top of Vesuvius, showing the funicular railway which they owned—the origin of the popular song 'Funiculi-Funicula'.

People able to enjoy this taste of travel wanted their friends at home to see something of the exotic places they were visiting just as they do today, and the new picture postcards made this possible.

In this way, the picture postcard craze quickly developed.

Germany was undoubtedly the centre of the picture postcard industry. Coloured picture postcards of places all over the world were printed in Berlin, and especially in Saxony and Bavaria. The business seems to have been largely controlled by Jewish interests, and they were undisputedly the exponents in the technique of colour printing of this sort. The Swiss were also producing excellent work, but they lacked the business initiative to market their knowledge, so that the Germans had the field all to themselves. The Germans established their agencies everywhere, and undercut all competitors. Most British postcard publishers ordered their coloured picture postcards from Germany, but some firms employed German workmen. In Scotland the firm of George Stewart of Edinburgh is thought to be one of the first in the British Isles to publish picture postcards in 1894 showing views.[1] Another famous Scottish business was the old established house of James Valentine and Sons of Dundee, who, in 1849, published many of the pictorial envelopes for Elihu Burritt's campaigns. In the years between they made a name for themselves with their high-class production of photographic views of landscapes and places of historic interest. Now, along with George Stewart of Edinburgh, Valentines were among the first to experiment with the new collotype process, a German invention for colour printing. In 1895 they applied this process to the manufacture of picture postcards, and quickly became one of the foremost picture postcard manufacturers in the United Kingdom.

[1] See Appendix VIII.

But, in general, manufacturers in Britain lagged far behind the Germans. The great hindrance was the square-shaped court card and the limit of size which prevented any illustration being printed to advantage. People, too, complained that cards of British manufacture fell far below the standard of continental cards. It was said that the innate conservatism of merchants and manufacturers prevented cards being up to the standard of foreign cards, and that they were not sufficiently attractive. Another objection was that cards were seldom sold singly, but always in packets, except when sold in the new penny-in-the-slot machines to be seen in the bigger and more important railway stations. Norman Alliston, writing in *Chambers's Journal* of October 21, 1899, remarked that "the illustrated post card is bound to become immensely popular in England, if only our apathetic designers, printers, and retail shopkeepers awake to the fact that profits will follow adequate commercial exploitation". The same writer described how in Germany cards were made of all shapes and sizes, some cards with panoramic views measuring 12 inches by 10, some depicting a view of the Rhine at Cologne, folding into three, and measuring over 16 inches in length. He described how, when a train stopped at a station, newspaper boys came hurrying along the platform peddling pictorial cards showing views of the town.

The craze for collecting picture postcards had now caught on in a big way, and on the Continent numerous picture postcard clubs and societies were forming, the members exchanging cards with members of postcard clubs in other countries. Cards were offered for sale everywhere, especially in the German-speaking countries where the craze for them was highest. In the cafés and open-air restaurants and other public places, it was common to see a postman with a mailing box strapped to his back, going from one table to the next, selling picture postcards and postage stamps. Then and there, people could write their messages and mail their postcards while the postman was waiting (see Frontispiece).

During 1899, international exhibitions of picture postcards took place in several continental cities. The first was held in Venice in August, later others took place in Nice and Ostend, then in Berlin, where one million postcards were posted from the exhibition hall, and another in Paris (Versailles), while a Cartophilic Congress was held in Prague. Cartophilia was the popular name coined for the new hobby of picture postcard collecting. Other names had been considered; cartomania was turned down, probably because the "mania" implied a more serious meaning, although a mania it certainly was. Cartography too, was suggested, but as this applied to the study of maps, cartophilia was finally decided on, until this too was gradually forgotten.

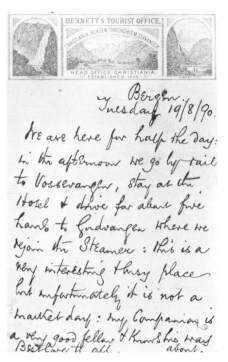

75. Bennett's Tourist Office postcard. Printed in brown. Dated 1890. (Reduced)

Thanks to the further efforts of Mr. Henniker Heaton, who had taken up the cause of the postcard publishers and the restricted size of postcards in 1899, this restriction was removed. The *Globe* in September of this year had this to say:

Mr. Henniker Heaton M.P. has received an unofficial communication to the effect that his request for the enlargement of the official inland post card has been granted, and that the change will take effect on November 1. Two cards—one white and the other buff—equal in size to the English foreign cards,

76. The halfpenny postcard used as an advertisement, 1885. (Reduced)

77. America's first pictorial postcards appeared for the World's Columbian Exhibition, Chicago, in 1893. (Reduced)

78. In Art Nouveau design, this card commemorates the 3rd International Exhibition of Art and 1st International Exhibition of Picture Postcards, held in Venice, August 1899. (Reduced)

will then be substituted for those at present in use. Messrs. De La Rue & Company are understood to have made many considerable concessions in the matter, which will result in a large saving to the Post Office. Another point pressed by the hon. member for Canterbury—that inland official post cards should be sold at the face value—has not yet been conceded.

Others, too, had presented arguments to the Postmaster General urging the removal of the restriction in size, among them Mr. Adolph Tuck of the firm of Raphael Tuck, who had set up in London early in the 1870s as manufacturers of greetings cards and became prominent for the very fine type of card they sold. Once the restriction limiting the size of postcards was removed, the firm of Tuck turned all the more to the publishing of picture postcards, and became well known for the highly artistic cards they produced.

The picture postcard craze had by now spread to the British Isles and is well described in an article that appeared in the *Standard* of August 21, 1899.

The illustrated postcard craze, like the influenza, has spread to these islands from the Continent, where it has been raging with considerable severity. Sporadic cases have occurred in Britain. Young ladies who have escaped the philatelic infection or wearied of collecting Christmas cards, have been known to fill albums with missives of this kind received from friends abroad; but now the cards are being sold in this country, and it will be like the letting out of waters. Many of them are "made in Germany" and imported, but home manufacture also has begun, or the foreign craftsman is adapting himself to English requirements. They have been taken up by the "penny-in-the-slot" general provider, and can be obtained at Kew and in other places of public resort which they illustrate. One enterprising firm seeks to arouse patriotism by picturing the vessels of the Navy.

Germany is a special sufferer from the circulation of these missives. The travelling Teuton seems to regard it as a solemn duty to distribute them from each stage of his journey, as if he were a runner in a paper chase. His first care on reaching some place of note is to lay in a stock, and alternate the sipping of beer with the addressing of postcards. Sometimes he may be seen conscientiously devoting to this task the hours of a railway journey. Would-be vendors beset the traveller on the tops of hills, and among the ruins of the lowlands, in the hotel, the *café*, and even the railway train. They are all over the country, from one end of the Fatherland to the other,—from the beech woods of Rügen on the North, to the southernmost summit in the Saxon Switzerland. Some of these cards, by the way, are of enormous size; and anyone in England who is favoured with them by foreign correspondents is subjected to a heavy fine by the inland postal authorities, who are not content with delivering them in a torn and crumpled state.

The illustrated post card has already gone through a process of evolution, and has developed species. The embryo was in existence more than half-a-century ago. Elderly people will remember the note-paper, headed with small engravings of scenery, which used to be sold at places where there was anything of special interest. Here was the germ of the idea. But the photograph came, and the illustrated note-paper disappeared. Then keepers of hotels and enterprising firms began to turn letter-paper and envelopes to advertising purposes, by suitable inscriptions in prominent type. That practice continues, as we all know; but it was not till the postcard was issued, now nearly thirty years ago, that this particular development became possible.

Postcards have one great advantage, that he who runs—or does not—may read, though we have heard of one being marked 'private'. It was not, however, till about five years ago, when any card of duly regulated size might be stamped and despatched through the post, that the illustrator and advertiser had really a chance, which they were not long in seizing. The results are legion, their varieties great. In some the illustration is subordinate to the advertisement; others are intended as memorials of places, and less expensive, if less accurate, than a photograph, of which, they are often transcripts. Another temptation is offered to the user. They are often so full of picture as to leave hardly any room for writing—which may be an equal blessing to the sender and receiver.

It is thanks to those who saved these early cards and formed collections, that collectors today have the pleasure

79. Britain's first picture postcards conformed to the regular Post Office size card. This example, brightly coloured, was printed in Germany. (Actual size)

and excitement of looking for them. These early cards have a distinctive charm, whether they are plain or coloured, and quite apart from the simple beauty of many of them and the interest they have in showing places and streets now very much altered, they provide nostalgic memories of a period which, by present-day standards, appears serene, gracious and secure.

Like an epidemic, the craze for saving postcards hit everyone, high and low, and Queen Victoria, who had shown a great interest in the development of the picture postcard, requested a royal relative to form a collection on her behalf.

In the United States postcards printed with pictorial advertisements had been for many years used commercially for advertising, and during the 1870s American greeting card publishers produced Christmas and New Year cards printed on the backs of the government postcards. But, officially, there were no pictorial postcards. The British Post Office restricted the use of both official and private postcards in a number of ways, until one by one the rules were gradually eased. In the United States the regulations governing the use of postcards were much more severe, and sometimes the Post Office went to extremes in order to stress the point they were making as, for instance, the simple rule governing the address side of the card. The first postcards carried the instruction: *Write the address only on this side—the message on the other.* This met with so much criticism that it was changed to: *Nothing but the address can be placed on this side.* This bit of humour was so palpable that the Post Office, acutely aware of its official dignity, tried again with, *Nothing but the address to be on this side.*

80. No. 1 of "The Postcard—The Smallest Monthly Journal in the World", issued March 1893. It was a method of using the postcard as an advertising medium. No other issues have been traced and it is a very scarce item. (Actual size)

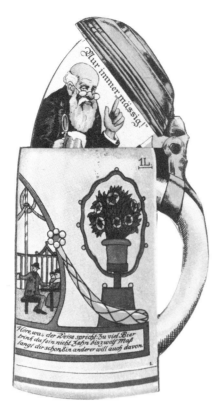

81. A postcard shaped like a beer-mug with a movable lid. Dated Vienna 1910. (Reduced)

But the public didn't like this somewhat terse order, so it was changed to, *This side is for address only*. The brevity of this seemed to spoil the precision of the sentence, so, finally, when new cards were prepared in 1874, the printed instruction read: *This side is for the address only* and, meeting with general approval, was retained.

Privately published picture postcards were not in general use in America until after the World Columbian Exposition of 1893, when, for the first time, coloured view cards of the Exhibition, handsomely printed, were placed on sale. Eventually, on May 19, 1898, an Act of Congress was passed allowing privately published postcards the same message privileges and rates as the government-issued cards; they were to be approximately the same size, quality and weight, and were to be inscribed "Private Mailing Card—Authorized by Act of Congress, May 19, 1898". American pictorial cards bearing a date before 1898 are indeed pioneer cards, and are hard to find. By reason of the Act of 1898, many publishers of cards set up in business, and, as was the case in Europe, the collecting of picture postcards became a raging hobby. New postal regulations came out on December 24, 1901, which stipulated that the words "Post Card" should appear at the top of the address side, as distinct from the government-issued cards, which would be designated "Postal Cards".

The urge to collect picture postcards among the French was triggered off by the visit of the Czar and the Russian Fleet at Toulon in October 1893, when an ornate postcard was issued to commemorate the event. Apart from this, and the Czar's other visits of a few years later, France issued few specially printed postcards until the Paris Exhibition of 1900, when several sets of beautifully printed postcards, delicately coloured, were produced for the occasion.

In Italy, picture postcards seem to have appeared about 1889. Usually printed in dark brown, they invariably showed a local view and one of the masterpieces of art from the local gallery. These early Italian cards are probably the first to show reproductions of works of art.

In Germany, Switzerland, Austria and the countries under Austrian rule, beautiful cards charmingly designed and in exciting colours were prolific. Novelties too, in the way of outsize cards and cards of unusual shape, were produced such as those on sale in the many fashionable spas, shaped like a mug, and others like a *stein*, with a movable top. So-called novelties—such as transparencies, cards to be held up against the light so that the picture changed, and others, with cut-out slits for windows, so that they appeared to be illuminated when shown against a light—delighted the tourists who bought them, firm in the belief that they were indeed novelties, although in actual fact they were but revivals of old ideas which had been the vogue a hundred years or more earlier.

Russia, Egypt, South America, the West Indies and many other far-away places were all customers for the German-made picture postcards. Exceptions were Japan, who produced delightful examples in her own typical style, and New Zealand where beautiful sets of views printed in London by Messrs. Waterlow and Sons were on sale. These were produced in a style quite different from most countries.

Beginning with exhibitions and shows, all sorts of events were commemorated on these early pictorial postcards, and consequently have provided truthful records of these occasions, which might not otherwise have been known. Events of topical interest too were quickly announced on postcards. In France, an interesting set of cards came out during 1898 publicizing the controversial Dreyfus case. In November 1899, comic cards were issued in Germany and Italy (and possibly in other countries too) showing the possible effect on the Earth when a comet was predicted to hit it. German examples prophesy something of an orgy, for ladies in partial undress are seen cavorting with their gentlemen friends who are decidedly the worse for liquor; they are shown trying to take cover in cupboards, under tables, and even in a trench dug in the garden! It was about now that the postcard was widely used for propaganda, when, in Germany, postcards were published of an anti-British nature, caricaturing and ridiculing Britain for her actions in South Africa during the Boer War.

At this early date, postcards were seldom vulgar, although at times rather suggestive in a harmless sort of way, but the humour depicted on them, especially on German and French cards, was sometimes low. The French Post Office in 1899 took steps to prevent obscenity on postcards passing through the post, and issued the following ambiguous instruction:

Employees are forbidden
  (a) to read postcards
  (b) to send, forward or deliver any postcard bearing written insults or abusive expressions.

While the Paris Exhibition helped a great deal to popularize the use of illustrated postcards (for until 1900 demand for them in France had not been very great) it was also the reason for a great many vulgar and obscene picture postcards being put on the market. Due to the influx of foreign visitors to Paris to see the Exhibition, there was a greater demand for picture postcards than ever before in the French capital. But at the same time it was found that the tourists were willing to buy all sorts of souvenirs, especially anything considered "naughty" or in any way suggestive, and

82. Cards of unusual shape went through the Austrian and German Post Offices without difficulty. Irregularly shaped cards were used in England about 1912–1914 but had only a short life as they embarrassed post office workers. Dated Carlsbad 1911. (Reduced)

supposedly typical of Paris. For this reason, numbers of very objectionable and obscene postcards were published. Public opinion and the feelings of the Parisians were aroused and disturbed by this, so measures were taken to suppress them. Commenting on this in an issue of *The Picture Postcard* in 1900, the writer says:

We are sure that no Post Office would forward such obscenity as is openly exhibited in the arcades of the Rue de Rivoli, or thrust into one's hands by itinerant newsvendors outside the cafés. It must be mentioned to the credit of the French Capital, however, that loud protests have been raised against this nuisance.

Attempts were made to stamp out the offensive practice when the Paris police raided all kiosks, tobacco and news shops and printers along the boulevards, at the Exhibition, and in every quarter of Paris where the nuisance prevailed. It is recorded that some 80,000 of these objectionable postcards were seized.

Because of an extraordinary "twist" in the minds of people, these postcards have now become collectors' items, and prices out of all proportion to their true worth are paid for them!

Picture postcards of a questionable sort were eventually on sale in many countries, those of German and Italian origin being especially suggestive and vulgar. In England too, during Edwardian years, it is surprising how many vulgar cards of English manufacture got through the post. People were so ashamed to show them that they were quickly destroyed, which is why, today, they are considered "rare"!

With the turn of the century, cards were published in many countries to mark the occasion. In Vienna, two interesting cards were issued in the form of cartoons. One depicts the things people were accustomed to in the 19th century, such as the currency in kreuzers and gulden; the invention of the postcard and a street lamp labelled "English Gas". The other, for the new century, shows the currency in hellers and kronen; the new electric tramway; an automobile; an airship; an express train; a tax on sugar; and a street lamp labelled "Communal Gas". An attractive Italian card depicts the new century by a symbolic young lady radiating rays of electricity from her outstretched arms, while a steaming railway engine tears along at great speed behind her. As a heading to the picture is printed "FINIS SAECULI XIX"

6

THE CRAZE FOR COLLECTING

WHEN Edward VII came to the throne the people in Britain enjoyed a very efficient and cheap postal service. To send a letter cost one penny for four ounces, and a postcard could be sent for a halfpenny. Anyone wanting to notify a friend in the town or near-by village that he or she would be coming over for a cup of tea in the afternoon had only to send a postcard by the morning's post to be sure of its delivery in time, for collections and deliveries were frequent. Telephones were not for everybody in those days, so that the halfpenny postcard was used extensively by everyone, and, judging by the huge quantities that have survived in the family postcard albums, it was the picture postcard that was popularly used. "Drop me a postcard" was said in just the same way that people today say "give me a ring".

Quite apart from its usefulness in conveying a quick message, the picture postcard was sent to please. Most people caught the craze for collecting them, and in many front rooms a picture postcard album was displayed for the admiration and interest of the caller. Every taste was catered for, and one's social standing could be determined by the style and quality of the picture postcards in the album. Architecture in the form of churches and cathedrals, castles and stately homes, reflected an aura of respectability, likewise the serene views of landscapes and pastoral scenes.

83. Printed in full colour by W. & A.K. Johnston Ltd. of Edinburgh, and dated 1902. The message on the card is of interest as it denotes the speed with which mail was attended to! (Reduced)

Foreign cards showing exciting views and glamorous pictures undoubtedly added to one's prestige; and there were the ordinary "family" cards, kept as souvenirs of one's holiday, or received from friends and relations.

To obtain foreign postcards for a collection was easy. There were many advertisements in the home journals and magazines which invited enquiries on a "pen-pal" basis. It is really extraordinary how these magazines circulated around the globe, because replies were received from picture postcard collectors all over the world. When old-time collections are studied it can be seen from the messages and addresses on the cards that they often emanate from postcard enthusiasts exchanging cards one with the other.

There were, besides, picture postcard clubs which were established in many Continental cities and towns, particularly in Germany and France. One of the more popular of these appears to have been the Kosmopolit, an extensive fraternity of enthusiastic picture postcard exchangers with members in most European countries and in the U.S.A. To promote the hobby still further were magazines and papers devoted exclusively to picture postcard collecting.

Germany had already shown how attractive picture postcards could be, with pictures of soldiers in dashing uniforms (an authority at the time stated that these cards were a great incentive to army recruiting), with pictures of the amenities offered by the fashionable spas, and by the many cards published in honour of Prince Bismarck, as well as by the huge variety of humorous cards, and it was easy to see the advertising potentialities in the brightly coloured picture postcards of hotels and restaurants.

The picture postcard trade was certainly booming. No sooner were the restrictions governing the size of postcards removed in 1899, than publishers were all in keen competition with each other. It was now that photography played a big part, and firms like Valentines of Dundee, who had made a name for themselves by their excellent photographic reproductions during the Victorian era, led the way with photographic views on postcards. Any number of firms sprang up almost overnight, all fighting one another by cutting prices for a share in the new boom.

An example of how quickly a business could grow is

64

GOOD WISHES FOR THANKSGIVING DAY.

shown by the firm of Wrench, publishers of the Wrench series. Evelyn Wrench was only 17 years of age in 1900, and having left Eton was "finishing" in Germany, where he was impressed with the good quality picture postcards he saw there, as compared with those he was used to in England. He considered the idea of starting a picture postcard business, selling view cards in England of the same fine finish and quality as those of German manufacture. The more he thought about it, the more enthusiastic he became, so that eventually his parents consented. Thereupon, he made arrangements with a firm of printers in Dresden, and, returning to London, he opened a one-roomed office in the Haymarket, in the same block now occupied by Burberrys. He began all alone, using a bicycle to get around London, seeing people and trying to get orders for his postcards. His next move was to engage an office boy named Conolly, and after the initial months of worry and uncertainty, a few orders started to come in. In his book *Uphill*,[1] Wrench describes how he and Conolly danced an Irish jig in the office on the morning his first big order for 50,000 cards came in. Young Wrench was fortunate in having good connections; his social standing gave him entrée to important people and because of this he was able to make arrangements with government departments, railway companies and very big concerns for the sale of his cards. He went to see Lady Warwick, who allowed the Wrench cards to be sold at Warwick Castle. He was among the first to have his post-

[1] *Uphill* by John Evelyn Wrench (Ivor Nicholson and Watson), 1934. Later, Sir Evelyn Wrench, the founder of the Royal Overseas League.

cards sold in the palaces and buildings controlled by the Office of Works, as well as the National Gallery, Westminster Abbey and the Tower of London. Today it is difficult to contemplate these show places without their picture postcards, but in 1900 they had none. Within four years Wrench had become a limited company, selling around £4,000 worth of cards a month, with a stock which ran into millions. From being a one-man concern, he now controlled a staff of 100. But his business had grown too rapidly. The firm received more orders than they could supply and ran into financial difficulties, so that early in 1904 the business was forced to close down.

The firm of Raphael Tuck entered into the market in a big way. They were already well known for the high standard and artistic merits of their greetings cards. Now they published some of the most beautiful picture postcards ever seen in the British Isles or, for that matter, anywhere. In 1900 they organized a competition, which was advertised on the backs of the packets of postcards published by them:

With a view of fostering the love of Art, and encouraging the collecting of artistic Post Cards, Prizes to the amount of £1000 will be awarded to the Collectors of the largest number of "TUCK'S POST CARDS" *that have passed through the post* no matter to whom addressed.

Every Post Card issued by us, either in Colour, Black and White, or "Real Photograph", whether VIEW, HEAD, FIGURE, EMPIRE, HERALDIC, ART, "WRITE-AWAY!", HUMOROUS, or whatever the subject may be, is eligible to compete so long as the name of our firm, and an impression of our Trade Mark (the Easel and Palette), appear on either side of the Post Card.

ssio Wireless Telegraph Station, Key West, Florida.

Anyone may compete, no entrance fee or charge of any kind being made.

Any number of Post Cards of the same design are eligible provided each one bears the postmark of a different date or of a different town. . .

Always use "Tuck's" Post Cards when writing to your friends, and advise them to carefully collect them, and in return to use "Tuck's" Post Cards when writing to you, so as to enable you to secure one of the PRIZES. . .

A few years later Tuck organized another scheme, the "snowball" idea, to help hospitals. People were asked to buy a packet of six Tuck's postcards and to join the postcard chain by sending them to their friends, asking them to do the same thing. There was a £1,000 gift to the hospital and a £50 prize to the winning entrant.

In January 1902 an important step forward for the use of pictorial postcards was made by the British Post Office when they took the initiative in allowing messages to be written on one half of the side reserved for the address, thereby leaving the whole of the other side to be taken up by the picture. Such cards, however, could not be sent abroad until other member countries of the Universal Postal Union had agreed to do the same. France was next to follow suit two years later, then Germany in 1905, and the United States in October 1907. It was not until June 1906 at a meeting of the Sixth Postal Union Congress in Rome that agreement was reached permitting the left half of the address side of postcards to be used for correspondence between U.P.U. members; it was also allowed to paste on an engraving or photograph, and to affix the postage stamp to the wrong side!

The usual price of a picture postcard was a penny. But cut-price competition among the publishers enabled old stocks to be cleared very cheaply. Tuck at one time offered cards at 16s. 6d. per 1,000, and a special offer of their famous "Oilette" series at five for a 1d., which usually sold at one penny each; 120 all different for 1s. 6d. was not unusual. Cards were often given away with copies of the popular weekly papers and magazines. The *Girl's Own Paper* published a very attractive series as a free issue in their paper, and the manufacturers of almost every household commodity, as well as the big stores, issued their own cards by way of advertisement. One of these, which today turns up more frequently than any other, is the famous "Bubbles", after the painting by Sir John Millais. This was produced by the manufacturers of Pears Soap and was sold for 6d. for a packet of twelve, or, to the trade, at 3d. These advertisement cards are much sought after today, in particular the very attractive cards published for every sort of theatrical performance. They hold nostalgic memories for all lovers of the theatre, and are invaluable to those engaged in theatrical research.

A unique series came out in 1905. This was *The Illustrated Daily Postcard*. With its title in Gothic face it resembled the front page of a daily newspaper, and was priced at one halfpenny. A black-and-white newsphoto was shown and the odd item of news.

86 (far left). A Valentine card dated 1907. Published by Messrs. Raphael Tuck. (Reduced)

87. An advertisement card issued by the National Telephone Company and used in 1907. (Reduced)

Propaganda, too, was carried on extensively by the means of postcards. They were used politically not only by contestants at election time, but also for the big campaigns such as the Suffragette movement, for Free Trade, and in support of Joseph Chamberlain. When Lloyd George introduced the National Health Insurance Act in 1911, one of the cards that were published showed the new stamp with the caption "This stamp will take a bit of licking". But the propaganda value of the postcard probably reached its highest level during the years of the First World War, when innumerable cards of poignant patriotic design were published as well as many striking examples of devotion to King and Country.

In order to be different and original, some publishers turned to so-called novelty and "trick" cards, though many were only imitations of what had been used in other ways during the early Victorian era. There were revolving discs, so that as the edge of the card was propelled by a finger, the centre-piece, divided into several panels, turned around, revealing a different picture with each turn. Another sort created a scintillating effect when the edge was turned. There were cards prettily ornamented with feathers, and cards with real hair fashioned on to the head of the beautiful lady depicted. Real satin or silk would be glued on to make a lady's dress, and often, on cards from Spain, matadors and Spanish beauties had their costume embroidered in bright silk thread, a custom still popular today in Spain as well as other countries.

Some cards were made of wood—a novelty used in

Austria during the 1890s, and later on in America. Some were made of birch bark, while an issue made in Hungary during 1899 has a neat frame in coloured mosaic upon the thin wooden card. Many cards were produced in the nature of toys, so that they squeaked when pressed, or opened up and changed into another form when handled in a certain way; things popped out, and a tongue would protrude when an overlap was pulled, or an arm or a leg would raise to make the picture amusing.

In Germany there were metachrome cards, which were coloured or otherwise printed. These were coated with a thin layer of white oil paint, making the view underneath look misty, but at the same time rendering it possible to use

88. Cards such as these were usually available on shipping services everywhere. (Reduced)

89. A well designed card printed in Paris. (Reduced)

90. A theatrical advertising card, printed in green and used in 1908. (Reduced)

the whole surface for writing. On receiving a card thus written on, the message was duly noted and the postcard laid in water, when, in a moment, the writing and mist entirely disappeared, leaving behind a charming view. Using a code or secret writing was popular in the early days of the postcard. An ingenious conception consisted of a numbered card perforated at regular intervals—this was placed over an ordinary postcard and the blank spaces written in; the code card had now to be turned, leaving other spaces to be filled in. A postcard written in this manner was quite indecipherable except to the recipient, who of course was supplied with the corresponding key-card.

From Ireland came cards made of peat-moss, which were part of a move to increase its use. From Canada and the U.S.A. came cards made of leather. Cards were even made out of a tin-like metal to which the Post Office objected on the grounds they could cause damage to other items of mail, so that they were required to be sent inside an envelope. Several charming sets of cards woven in silk were published during the early years of the century, and again during World War I, when not only woven silk cards but cards embroidered in coloured silks having patriotic emblems and sentimental messages were made in France and proved very popular with the troops.

Among the favourites were the Transparencies—cards which, when held against a bright light, transformed into a different picture.

All these types of cards were popular, and each country had its speciality. The English silk cards were mostly made in Coventry, some by T. Stevens who for years had specialized in this kind of work. But other firms made them too. Cards with woven flowers came from Austria and Switzerland, and almost all the novelty and "trick" cards were made in Germany. In this respect it is interesting to note how Germany catered for the tastes of nearly the whole world, and how all countries liked much the same thing. We find the same sort of sentimental card was popular everywhere. Royalty and prominent people were popular in all countries. Much the same sort of humour was enjoyed and understood in all languages. Lovely ladies were everywhere considered beautiful, regardless of nationality.

No time was lost in recording some special event or an accident; a royal visit or the unveiling of a monument was quickly published and the postcards immediately made available. When the King and Queen visited Dublin on July 8, 1911, a photograph of the event was taken at about 10.30 in the morning. This was processed, a half-tone block was made and the postcard was printed on the same day. Furthermore, a special dated postmark reading "Dublin Castle" was used for the occasion. Whenever a train crashed, a tram car turned over, a ship became stranded on

91

92

93

91. Numerous postcards were published during the period of the Suffragettes, both for and against the movement.

92. Lloyd George and the National Health Stamp, 1911.

93. Patriotic postcards were published for every occasion. This one celebrated the Coronation of 1911.

94. Even Royalty were used in advertising.

(All reduced)

94

G*

95. The Sydney Street Siege, 1911. An example of the practice of recording current events on postcards. (Reduced)

96. An aeroplane crash, July 17, 1913. Local events were immediately depicted on postcards. (Reduced)

97. King Edward VII off for a drive in 1903. (Reduced)

the rocks, or an aeroplane fell into the branches of a tree, the local photographer was there on the spot, and in very quick time a picture postcard recorded the occasion. In this way we have factual descriptions of the earthquakes and landslides, floods, fires and disasters that occurred in all parts of the world. The picture postcard has always faithfully recorded what has happened and nowadays these old postcards give us views of our cities and towns as they used to be, especially those which suffered the air raids of the last war. We learn that London's streets could be very crowded in King Edward's time, and were as difficult to cross as they are today. We see congestion of horsedrawn buses, hansom cabs, and carts and drays of all descriptions.

Picture postcards reveal that when people went out for the day they put on their best clothes. People walking along the Hove Lawns or the sea-front at Scarborough look smartly dressed, the ladies with their parasols, feathered hats and lacy skirts, the gentlemen wearing straw hats and Sunday-best suits, and nearly always carrying a walking stick. The crowd scenes of the many exhibitions that took place during King Edward's reign show this very forcibly. People "dressed-up" for the occasion. Some twenty years later, at Wembley Exhibition, it is interesting to note the changed aspect of the crowd, and again, in 1951 at the Festival of Britain Exhibition on the South Bank: the people are seen to be dressed only casually. Few men or women are wearing hats, and the scene lacks the graciousness of earlier days.

Suburban street scenes too show how things have changed. The row of Victorian villas looks much the same, but the milkman with his milk cart on which a large

98. A charming design embellished with real feathers. (Reduced)

brass churn stands is now unfamiliar. The horsedrawn carriages and the odd-looking motor-car parked on the side of the road make it a "period" picture. Often a suburban or village Post Office is shown, with the postman wearing his shako type cap, standing beside his bicycle. Postmen in those days seemed always to favour a drooping moustache. Postcards showing shops can be fascinating. The arrangement of the window display (usually very crowded), the sort of things offered, and the large gas lamps along the top of the signboard, hold one's attention. By taking a reading glass, the price tickets can be seen and other details discovered.

Transport was often featured on these early postcards. Warships, ocean liners, paddle steamers and the little steamers that cruised around the coast and up the rivers are all recorded. All types of trains, from the crack expresses and boat trains to the little Mumbles tram at Swansea. Accurate details are shown of the horse trams, which were followed first by the steam trams and then by the electric trams. Some cards show the inauguration of a city's tram service with the mayor dressed in morning coat and top hat at the controls, and the entire car filled with top-hatted aldermen and city dignitaries, with their wives. The horse buses make a brave showing, especially those depicted in colour. There was keen competition among the different bus companies in those days, and, like the mail and stage coaches of a century earlier, they all had names, painted in large letters along the sides, such as "Union Jack", "Pioneer", "Vanguard", "Arrow", to name only a few. In due course they were followed by the first motor buses, looking rather top heavy on their narrow, solid-tyred wheels.

Although many of these pictures of transport look comical by modern standards, they were regarded at the time with the same interest as is shown today in the latest racing car or diesel engine. Much of the charm attaching to picture postcards of the Edwardian era is intangible. The pictures recall nostalgic memories to those who lived through those times, by showing the style and fashion of a more leisurely period in our history, when graciousness and courtesy were understood and appreciated by every class of person. At the same time they hold an attraction for younger people who have never known this way of life. Today, when an Edwardian picture postcard is held in the hand, time for the moment is captured; for the picture is not just a reproduction or copy such as can be seen in a book, but is an actual representation of that time, and is something belonging to those years.

Having this perception anyone can enjoy looking at picture postcards which might otherwise appear ludicrous to some people. Pictures of ardent lovers, stiffly posed with dramatic gestures and gazing fixedly into each other's eyes;

99. A corner of Tottenham Court Road, London, in 1909. (Reduced)

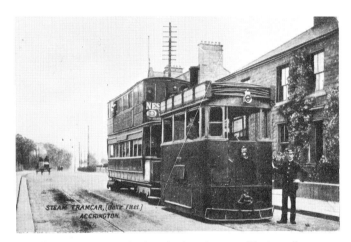

100. A steam tramcar in Accrington, Lancs. (Reduced)

101. Best clothes were always worn on Sundays. The Hove Lawns with West Pier Brighton in the background, in 1908. (Reduced)

102

103

Merry Christmas Greetings

QUEEN OF THE CARNIVAL.

104

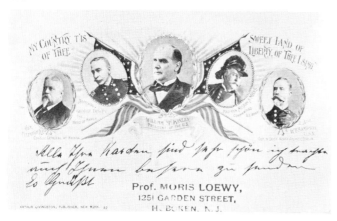

Prof. MORIS LOEWY,
1251 GARDEN STREET,
HOBOKEN, N. J.

105

H.R.H. THE PRINCE OF WALES.

106

Ostende Baigneurs

102. One of the first London motor buses on a postcard of 1906.

103. A Tuck greeting card of 1907.

104. Private Mailing card, published by Arthur Livingston, New York, in 1898, printed in red and blue.

105. A popular portrait of H.R.H. the Prince of Wales.

106. Bathers at Ostend, 1903.
(All reduced)

bathing beauties wearing costumes with wide stripes and trousers finishing below the knees; angelic children looking, by today's standards, utterly revolting, dressed in Little Lord Fauntleroy suits, or wearing nothing at all (and still looking nauseating). Every sort of cat imaginable, posed in baskets, in tea-cups, under parasols, in flower-pots, wearing sun bonnets and having tea parties. These cards were not meant to be laughed at, but they are enjoyed today because they are so fantastic.

Humorous cards appeared right from the start, printed on the court-sized cards. They showed a black-and-white sketch in one corner, and repeated exactly the same sort of humour which was shown on note-paper of 1840-1842, for example a tramp sitting on a fence ruminating, bearing the sentence beginning: "Business is so brisk that . . ." Tuck used this notion (but printed in colour) in their popular series of "write-away" cards. They were so successful that many other publishers brought out similar sets. But most surprising of all early comic cards were those which were published in about 1902 printed in black and white from the identical blocks used by Rock and Co. of London, in their comic note-paper series of the 1850s!

In Scotland, Messrs. Cynicus of Fife was one of the earliest firms to specialize in comic cards. They developed a distinctive style of their own, and would appear to have pioneered the idea of designs which could be overprinted with many different local captions.

Many early comic cards were drawn by well-known artists; John Hassall, who designed posters, was one, and had already made a name for himself on the staff of *Punch*. Another *Punch* artist was Tom Browne, who will always be remembered for his early seaside comic postcards, quite apart from his portrayal of humorous episodes in the day of the ordinary household, along with fat cooks and police-men, parlour maids and soldiers, henpecked husbands never able to do anything right, and be-goggled motorists always in trouble on the road.

Scenes at the seaside had always been a popular theme ever since they were first depicted on writing paper in the 1850s, and subsequently in sets of cartes-de-visite. Now, in all countries, this source of humour was used on picture postcards. Inevitably, the seaside comic postcard with its picture of mixed bathing, along with a distinctive exaggeration of the human form, sometimes lent itself to a certain amount of vulgarity. A young artist named Donald McGill in the early years of the century quickly became known for his comic postcards which, although never downright obscene, sometimes had a suggestive sense of vulgarity about them which has ever since been associated with the English seaside and typifies an aspect of English life and humour.

Artists such as Phil May, Harry Payne and Lawson Wood

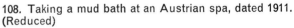

107. Cards such as this in 1910 were not intended to be comic! (Reduced)

108. Taking a mud bath at an Austrian spa, dated 1911. (Reduced)

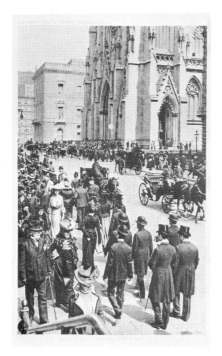

109. Fifth Avenue, New York, in 1909 (Reduced)

110. A romantic episode from New Jersey 1910. (Reduced)

111. A typical Bamforth sentimental card used in 1905. (Reduced)

contributed their own distinctive brand of humour, in particular Louis Wain, whose famous cats are beloved by everyone, and are favourites among collectors; while others, like Lance Thackeray, owed their fame to the postcard. Popular today too, with some collectors of humorous postcards of the Edwardian period, are the Bamforth comics. The Bamforth business was founded at Holmfirth in Yorkshire during the 1860s by James Bamforth, who was a maker of lantern slides. His speciality was to paint a backcloth and photograph living models against it, actually using his own employees for the purpose, with perhaps one or two "extras" brought in from the neighbourhood. In later years his son Edwin developed the postcard side of the business and carried on the same technique. This firm became famous also for their "Song and Hymn" postcards. These, consisting as a rule of from 2 to 4 cards in a set, were heavily sentimental and full of pathos; they were intended to touch the heart deep down and included such titles as: "Rocked in the Cradle of the Deep", "Mamma Number Two", "Heroes of the Mine" and dozens more.

To make these photographs, people were posed against a painted background with "props" which were kept for the purpose or sometimes borrowed locally. It is said that the Bamforth staff enjoyed these events when they had to dress up and be photographed, and small children, brought in for the occasion, were usually rewarded with sweets.

During the 1914-1918 war Bamforths published similar sentimental sets showing loved ones leaving home for the front, sweethearts left behind dreaming about them, sorrowing parents and lonely graves. The great feature about all of Bamforth's cards was the sort of highly emotional verse which accompanied the pictures. They were indeed "tear-jerkers", which many people would be prone to describe as "slush". Today, Bamforths are foremost among the publishers of the so-called comic seaside picture postcards.

Comic cards were of course also imported from the Continent, especially those which showed scenes of flirting and courting, but one type in particular for some peculiar reason was much in demand. This type showed groups of babies and small children usually with very little clothing, dressed in only their vests and often in the nude, and always posed in a variety of extraordinary postures. They were always depicted doing the same things together, such as performing in a band concert, washing and laundering, crowded in a motor-car together, or packed tightly in an airship. They would be shown as the hearts of cabbages in a field, and again, being gathered up and delivered as ordered. They were made to portray every sort of whim and occasion—even one, entitled "A Public Sitting", when they are all shown sitting on their potties! These cards were usually in colour and, by photo-montage, actual photographs of babies were superimposed over drawings.

This technique of photo-montage, whereby photographs

were superimposed upon others, enabled many striking and extraordinary subjects to be shown. A popular series were the "Capital Letters", or "Initials"; cherubic looking children would be placed in the most impossible and absurd positions as part of the background or to help fashion a part of the letter, where as a rule a beautifully gowned lady would be standing.

An American artist from Massachusetts named Charles Dana Gibson made a hit in 1903 with a series of humorous drawings which portrayed and made famous a tall, disdainful yet mischievous-looking girl, whose type became known as the "Gibson Girl" and was typified by the actress Camille Clifford. Her song "Why do they call me a Gibson Girl?" was a great success in *The Belle of Mayfair* at the Vaudeville Theatre in 1906.

Postcards portraying female models, sometimes in tights or swathed in a clinging type of garment, appeared around 1901 in Paris. They were imported into England described as "French Actresses". Considered rather daring, they were photographically produced in black and white, sometimes tinted a little. The next year, similar cards were produced in England, printed in monochrome in glamorous shades of colour. Doubtless the popularity of this kind of card paved the way for the portrayal of stage celebrities. During 1904 several series of postcards of famous actresses and actors were published which were highly successful; they are a permanent reminder of the English stage as it was during the Edwardian era. So avidly were they collected, and published in such quantity, that large numbers of them have survived, in spite of the clearances made during two World Wars through salvage campaigns and other destructive measures.

Here are portrayed all the famous names of the theatre, names like Henry Irving, Sarah Bernhardt and Ellen Terry, and idols such as Marie Lloyd, Vesta Tilley and Gertie Millar, as well as a whole host of others whose names today are well remembered and known even by many of this present generation.

Bearing in mind there was no cinema, the stage in those days was nearer to the people than it is today, and it is understandable why these theatrical stars were the heroes and heroines of so many. In truth, they really had a public, and the public gave them its affection. Many of these stars featured differently on picture postcards several times over. Marie Studholme, it is said, was the most photographed British actress of all. The Rotary Photo Company, one of the largest publishers of theatrical personalities, produced over a hundred studies of her, and she was portrayed by other publishers too. It has been scathingly alleged that stars such as she spent more time in the photographic studios than on the stage! Edna May, Mabel Love and Gabrielle

112. The Kaiser with his six sons. A card posted from Berlin, 1914. (Reduced)

113. Vesta Tilley, the famous Music Hall artiste, in 1911. (Reduced)

Ray were among the "top ten" for popularity; then came the Dare sisters, Phyllis and Zena, who were photographed in all sorts of styles, and enjoyed a long reign of affection. Probably among the last to be idolized in this way on postcards was Gladys Cooper in the 1920s.

Interesting experiments were made on these photographic studies early in the century by attempts at colouring, but, by and large, real photographs in black and white were preferred. A new technique was undertaken by the Philco Publishing Co. in 1904 on their series of theatrical stars when they introduced from the Continent what was regarded as an innovation. This was the decoration by means of tinselling, or "jewelling" as it was known in the trade. This differed very little from the spangled theatrical prints of the 1830s. Jewelling was also applied to view

114. One of a popular series "La premiere violette", by Raphael Kirchner. (Reduced)

115. From the Series *San Toy*, designed by Raphael Kirchner. (Reduced)

cards, the principal buildings or main parts of the picture being pricked out with little sparklers of different colours. When used for greetings and birthday cards this form of decoration was very effective. But the postage required to be double, one penny instead of a halfpenny, because the rule was that anything stuck on to a card rendered it liable to double postage.

Studies of pretty ladies, as would be expected, were published in all countries. Some, more daring than others and considered "saucy", usually came from Paris, and several exceptionally charming series came from Berlin and Vienna. Today the sets designed by Raphael Kirchner are keenly sought after. In 1901 Kirchner depicted young ladies gracefully posed, sometimes clothed in a form of negligée, but always discreet. His style was entirely different from the usual and his work was received with enthusiasm, particularly the sets of cards published in London featuring the musical plays of *San Toy* and *The Geisha* and Gilbert and Sullivan's opera *The Mikado*. A year or so later appeared his series 'Les Cigarettes du Monde' when his own particular type of feminine beauty was shown in somewhat more daring postures. From now on he drew his young ladies in rather suggestive poses, often partially clothed or coyly showing their charms. They were typically daring in an Edwardian sense and were considered a trifle risqué, but were so exquisitely drawn and shown in such delightful colouring that they have survived—although not always in the family albums. Many of his more provocative designs appeared during the First World War when they were obviously intended to cheer and amuse the troops at the front.

Kirchner was contemporary with a new style of artistic design now becoming popular, which was apparent on many cards of continental manufacture. Perhaps the most prominent exponent of "Art Nouveau" was a young Czech artist, Alphonse Mucha, who made his name in Paris with his theatrical posters, his most famous being those for Sarah Bernhardt. His designs, along with others of his contemporaries, were eventually reproduced on postcards, and are now greatly prized by collectors. They belong to "la belle époque", a period of bohemian charm, essentially Parisian. Around 1904, Raphael Tuck published a few series of "Art Nouveau" postcards which are probably appreciated far more today than they were at the time, for not nearly so many of these are to be found, whereas those of Tuck's "Connoisseur" series, depicting a range of beautiful women painted by Asti, seem to be plentiful.

This era of the picture postcard is superbly described by James Douglas, the prominent London journalist. Writing in 1907 he says:

When the archaeologists of the thirtieth century begin to ex-

117

116

118

119

Du kennst mein Herz noch lange nicht!-

120

Im Prater.

116. Some Louis Wain cats, 1906.

117. A card by Tom Browne, dated 1905.

118. A popular seaside series. Pebbles, fish, shrimps or shells were cleverly arranged for this sort of design.

119. A flirtatious design, Art Nouveau style, used in 1906.

120. A design in modern style. Posted from Vienna in 1909. (All reduced)

"Toutes mes prières sont pour vous."

121. Published by Noyer of Paris about 1918. 'Les petites femmes de Paris.'

122. Published by Noyer of Paris. A war-time card.

123. A Tuck "Write Away" card used in 1903. Drawn by Lance Thackeray. The same idea was used on comic notepaper in 1841.

124. Lovely ladies have always been a popular subject on postcards the world over.

(All reduced)

cavate the ruins of London, they will fasten upon the Picture Postcard as the best guide to the spirit of the Edwardian era. They will collect and collate thousands of these pieces of pasteboard, and they will reconstruct our age from the strange hieroglyphs and pictures that time has spared. For the Picture Postcard is a candid revelation of our pursuits and pastimes, our customs and costumes, our morals and manners. It is not easy to discover the creator of the Picture Postcard. He has been swallowed by oblivion. It is a pity that his lineaments should remain unknown. If we were not careless custodians of our own greatness, we should have erected a colossal statue of this nameless benefactor, so that posterity might gaze upon his features and ponder on the cut of his frock coat.

Like all great inventions, the Picture Postcard has wrought a silent revolution in our habits. It has secretly delivered us from the toil of letter-writing. There are men still living who can recall the days when it was considered necessary and even delightful to write letters to one's friends. Those were times of leisure. Our forefathers actually sat down and wasted hours over those long epistles which still furnish the industrious bookmaker with raw material. It is said that there is at this moment in London several tons of unpublished letters by Ruskin, and it is alleged that a few hundredweights from the pen of Robert Louis Stevenson have not yet seen the light. It is sad to think of the books that dead authors might have written if they had saved the hours which they squandered upon private correspondence. Happily, the Picture Postcard has relieved the modern author from this slavery. He can now use all his ink in the sacred task of adding volumes to the noble collection in the British Museum. Formerly, when a man went abroad he was forced to tear himself from the scenery in order to write laborious descriptions of it to his friends at home. Now he merely buys a picture postcard at each station, scribbles on it a few words in pencil, and posts it. This enhances the pleasures of travel.

Many a man in the epistolary age could not face the terrors of the Grand Tour, for he knew that he would be obliged to spend most of his time in describing what he saw or ought to have seen. The Picture Postcard enables the most indolent man to explore the wilds of Switzerland or Margate without perturbation.

Nobody need fear that there is any spot on the earth which is not depicted on this wonderful oblong. The photographer has photographed everything between the poles. He has snapshotted the earth. No mountain and no wave has evaded his omnipresent lens. The click of his shutter has been heard on every Alp and in every desert. He has hunted down every landscape and seascape on the globe. Every bird and every beast has been captured by the camera. It is impossible to gaze upon a ruin without finding a Picture Postcard of it at your elbow. Every pimple on the earth's skin has been photographed, and wherever the human eye roves or roams it detects the self-conscious air of the reproduced. The aspect of novelty has been filched from the visible world. The earth is eye-worn. It is impossible to find anything which has not been frayed to a frazzle by photographers.

The human face has fared like the human earth. It has been stamped on pasteboard so many times in so many ways that it has lost its old look of unawareness. It has grown common. There is no facial expression left which affects one with the

125. A Bamforth card of 1904. (Reduced)

126. 'Workers unite—and be masters of the world.' A political card from Italy, May 1, 1903. (Reduced)

127

127. This card, designed by Alphonse Mucha and printed in light green and yellow, was posted in 1901.

128. A German bathing beauty of 1909.

129. Numerous sets of cards showing the world's postage stamps were published in Germany during the early part of the century.

130. A fine example in Art Nouveau—a card honouring Czar Nicholas II of Russia for initiating the Disarmament Conference in 1898—published in Venice. This was issued in different languages for several countries.

131. An embossed card published by Robbins of Boston, Mass., in 1908.

(All reduced)

128

129

130

131

132. German publishers produced cards showing the coinages of many countries, embossed and in colour. (Reduced)

133. "Declarations of War are taken in here—only don't shove there are more to come." Postmarked August 28, 1914, from Munich. (Reduced)

sensation of surprise. The ingenious efforts of actresses have familiarized the youngest office boy with all the mysteries of beauty. It is no longer possible to discover a new kind of smile. There are not many varieties of smile within the compass of our facial muscles. At any rate, the Picture Postcard seems to suggest that there are not more human smiles than human jokes. It is said that there are only three distinct jokes in the world. It is certain that there are not more than two smiles. The most accomplished professional beauty can smile in only two ways. She can smile with her mouth open and she can smile with her mouth shut. The Picture Postcard has accustomed us to the charms of both smiles. . . .

The Postcard has always been a feminine vice. Men do not write Postcards to each other. When a woman has time to waste, she writes a letter; when she has no time to waste, she writes a Postcard. There are still some ancient purists who regard Postcards as vulgar, fit only for tradesmen. I know ladies who would rather die than send a Postcard to a friend. They belong to the school which deems it rude to use abbreviations in a letter, and who consider it discourteous to write a numeral. The Postcard is, indeed, a very curt and unceremonious missive. It contains no endearing prefix or reassuring affix. It begins without a prelude and ends without an envoy. The Picture Postcard carries rudeness to the fullest extremity. There is no room for anything polite. Now and then one can write on a blue sky or a white road, but, as a rule, there is no space for more than a gasp. . . .

Dr. Heinrich von Stephan's suggestion in 1865 for the use of a small piece of card to send openly through the post with only a few written words on it, instead of a lengthy letter with all its formalities, was indeed proved to be right, but he little knew to what extent his idea was to change the social aspect and writing habits of almost everyone in the world.

Today, the picture postcard is still the best and most favoured means of keeping in touch. Upon arrival in a distant place, or whilst on holiday, a picture postcard is usually sent off to remind friends and acquaintances that they are not forgotten, and many a picture postcard is cherished for sentimental or romantic reasons. Sending a postcard has often saved or preserved a friendship over the years, and has prevented families and friends from losing touch with one another.

The idea of the postcard can truthfully be said to have been one of the most useful creations of all times.

APPENDIX I

LIPMAN'S POSTAL CARDS

Earliest known of any postcards are the private cards for which John P. Charlton of Philadelphia obtained a copyright in 1861. The copyright was later transferred to H. Lipman, also of Philadelphia, who printed and sold a plain message card bearing the inscription in the top left corner "Lipman's Postal Card". Printed beneath in two lines of small lettering is: *Patent applied for. Entered according to Act of Congress in the year 1861 by J. P. Charlton, Phila. in the Clerk's Office of the District Court of the U.S. for the Eastern District of Penna.* Only four of these cards are known, none of them postally used. A second issue of the card was printed with a squared space for a postage stamp and address lines on one side, with the back of the card left blank for messages or advertisements; a slightly ornamental border in twisted line surrounded the entire design in either red, blue, or green.

The earliest recorded date of one of these cards postally used is October 25, 1870. Lipman's Postal Cards are doubtless the first cards ever to be called "postal cards" and under the United States Postal Act of February 27, 1861, which fixed a one cent rate (to be prepaid by a postage stamp) they are the first cards ever to be officially allowed for postal purposes, which gives the United States priority over Europe where the invention of the postcard is concerned. They were actually on sale and used until 1873, when the first government postal cards appeared.

134. A Lipman's Postal Card, used in October 1870. Reproduced by courtesy of Mr. Charles A. Fricke of Philadelphia. (Reduced)

APPENDIX II

THE WORLD'S FIRST POSTCARDS

Under the title *Uber eine neue Art der Korrespondenz mittels der Post* (A new way of correspondence by post), Dr. Emanuel Herrmann, professor of political economy at the Military Academy of Wiener-Neustadt, published an article in the *Neue Freie Presse* on January 26, 1869, in which he discussed the financial burden to the State brought about by postal correspondence. He divided this correspondence into three groups according to their contents:

(1) Letters with ordinary information
(2) Business letters and spiritual information
(3) Love and family letters.

Dr. Herrmann came to the conclusion that the letters mentioned in group (1) with ordinary contents such as despatch notices, receipts, accounts, orders, short commercial announcements, as well as the vast amount of personal greetings letters for the New Year and other special occasions, amounted to roughly one-third of the total bulk of the mail. It was for this type of correspondence that Herrmann proposed a means for cutting down expense. He suggested that the government should introduce cards the size of envelopes with writing space to contain not more than twenty words of handwriting or print, to be sent through the post openly, franked with a 2 Kreuzer value, in just the same way as an ordinary letter at the 5 Kreuzer rate. The public would save millions of Gulden on postage and letter-writing material, and the Post Office would benefit by the increase in mail.

The Postmaster General, Baron von Maly, thought very well of the idea and at once saw its usefulness. He contacted Dr. Herrmann and suggested that a 3 Kreuzer postage might serve instead, for a folded card, the size of an octavo letter sheet, regardless of the number of words. Later, this too was adopted and was introduced in 1886 as a "Karten-Brief" (Letter Card).

Dr. Herrmann's proposals were accepted in full and on September 22, 1869, a Post Office Regulation No. 21.18.916. 1832 proclaimed:

Regarding the introduction of correspondence cards for internal communication.

In agreement with the Royal Hungarian Secretary of Commerce, the Postal Department will issue correspondence cards, starting October 1 of this year, according to the details given below. They will be used for short written communications to all places of the Austro-Hungarian Monarchy regardless of distance and will require a uniform fee of two (2) Neukreuzer (new Kreuzer).

The following regulations will direct the sale of these cards, as to the way they are to be used for writing and how they are to be handled:

1. The correspondence cards with their imprinted value can be bought at all post offices and in all postage stamp outlets at the price of two (2) Neukreuzer a piece. They are to be mailed openly, without any seal whatsoever.

2. Just like letters, they will have to carry the exact address, consisting of first name and family name of the addressee, the place of destination, and, unless it is a poste restante address, also the full street address.

Following the place of destination the name of the province has to be given and also the county, if several places have the same name. If the place has not its own post office, the post office has to be named to which it is subordinated.

The address has to appear on the front side of the card.

3. The back of the card is to be used for the written message. It can be written with ink, pencil, colour pencil, etc., but care should be taken that the writing is legible and durable.

4. For the time being these cards can be sent to all places of the Austro-Hungarian Monarchy and, just like letters, they have to be mailed in the same way.

They can be registered against payment of the regular registration fee and the stamps for the registration have to be affixed on the back of the card, next to the wording: "Space for written information".

5. No additional fee is necessary for forwarding a postcard to another inland place, different from the one indicated on the address, nor for returning it to the sender.

6. For places that are not serviced by an official letter carrier one (1) additional Neukreuzer for the delivery will be charged extra.

7. The Post Department will not be responsible for the contents of the message. Nevertheless the post offices are instructed, similar to an order existing for letters that carry offensive remarks in the address (postal regulation of March 8, 1865) to exclude postcards likewise from transportation and delivery, if obscenities, libellous remarks or other punishable acts are found on the cards.

8. Postcards which have become useless by error or chance before being mailed, can be exchanged against payment of 1 Neukreuzer in the same way and under the same conditions, which regulate the exchange of spoiled envelopes with imprinted stamps.

9. The Imperial and Royal Postal Departments are to take notice of the above regulations and must observe the following directions:

(a) Each post office as well as all postage stamps retailers have to keep in stock a normal supply of imprinted correspondence cards at all times. These will be furnished by the stamp depots in packets bundled at 50 each and are to be handled and inventoried just like envelopes with imprinted stamps.

The sale of postcards must start on October 1st of this year.

(b) Cards that have been mailed are to be treated during the sorting process, transportation and delivery just like letters that carry stamps.

In particular the cancellation of the imprinted and possibly other stamps on the cards has to be done according to the existing regulations.

If a number of postcards is mailed at a post office, they are to be tied and sorted, separately from the letters, but registered postcards are to be turned in together with registered letters.

Postcards in transit are not to be cancelled, but the arrival postmark is to appear on the front of the card on the left side, opposite the imprinted stamp.

Vienna, September 22, 1869

Paragraphs 4 and 7 of these regulations are particularly interesting, because the cards carried instructions on them printed in the German language only—"Space for written messages" and "The Post Office will not be responsible for the contents of the message". This caused resentment and anger in all the Slavonic areas of the Austro-Hungarian Monarchy where German was not spoken, especially in those parts where there was a strong Nationalist tendency, and the Austrian Government was compelled to issue new postcards under an order of September 8, 1871, in bilingual text "for those postal districts, in which another language besides German is used". They were:

(a) Postal District Lemberg: German-Polish, German-Ruthenian (in Cyrillic letters)

(b) Postal District Prague: German-Czech

(c) Postal District Brünn: German-Czech, German-Polish

(d) Postal District Graz: German-Slovenic

(e) Postal District Trieste: German-Slovenic, German-Italian

(f) Postal District Innsbruck: German-Italian

(g) Postal District Zara: German-Italian

A few years later cards were also printed with Rumanian and Illyric texts.

A picture of the Abbey of Melk in Lower Austria is reported on a postcard of the 1869-71 issue (with the German text), but its actual origin and date are obscure.[1] It might well be that this was printed on old stock of the 1869-71 issue at some later date, for the same illustration is known on later issues. For it was not until 1881 that a Postal Regulation was issued permitting imprinted illustrations and pictorial advertising on the backs of postcards. On December 12, 1884, it was allowed for private enterprise to print and publish pictorial postcards, which, of course, required to be franked by a 2 Kreuzer postage stamp. At the same time it was strictly forbidden to affix any sort of illustration by pasting, or embossing; this was because cards had been privately produced in this way with stuck-on

[1] Reported by Franz Hutter of the Heimatsmuseum in Melk, Austria.

portraits of Czech nationalists and embossed heraldic emblems, patriotic mottoes, and other additions of a political demonstrative character.

An interesting variety of the Austrian postcard exists in the form of an error of printing, which appeared on the Bohemian issue in November 1873. A 5 Kreuzer value in yellow was printed in error instead of the 2 Kreuzer. To overcome this mistake, the Post Office authorities affixed a 2 Kreuzer postage stamp (which was of the same colour and design) over the erroneously printed value.

APPENDIX III

THE FIRST BRITISH POSTCARD

Designed, printed and manufactured by Messrs. De la Rue and Company, Great Britain's first postcards were on sale October 1, 1870, authorized by the Post Office Act of 1870, which stated that:

Pursuant to an Act passed in the last session of Parliament (33 and 34 Vict. c. 79), POST CARDS have been prepared for correspondence by Post in the United Kingdom after the 30th of the present month, stamped with the postage duty of one halfpenny.

These cards will be sold without any charge beyond the duty. A single card or any number of cards may be purchased, but they will be sent out from this office in packets containing twenty-four cards, price 1s., and in parcels of twenty packets, price £1. They may be obtained at all Post-offices, and from licensed vendors of stamps.

The cards will be also supplied when required in sheets containing forty-two cards, and measuring about $29\frac{5}{8}$ by $21\frac{1}{2}$. Although the cards may thus be obtained in sheets for the purpose of affording facility for printing upon them, each card must afterwards be separated from the sheet, as no combination of cards can pass through the Post-office.

Such sheets will be issued only in half-reams, containing 240 sheets (10,080 cards), duty £21, and will be supplied to the public at the Inland Revenue Offices in London, Edinburgh, and Dublin, and at the offices of the distributors and sub-distributors of stamps in the country. A discount of 4s. per half-ream will be allowed to purchasers. . . .

Post cards cannot be used before the 1st October.

Those made up in packets will not be sold before that date;

but cards in sheets will be supplied by this office on and after 26th instant, to enable the public to print on them preparatory to their use next month.

It is desirable that persons requiring cards in sheets should make early application for them.

By order of the Board,
(Signed) T. SARGENT, *Secretary*.

Inland Revenue, Somerset House,
9th September, 1870.

APPENDIX IV

PRIVATELY PRINTED POSTCARDS

In June, 1872, the Postmaster General issued the following notice: [1]

Notice is hereby given, that on and after the 17th June private cards may be taken to the office of the Inland Revenue to be impressed with a halfpenny stamp under conditions which may be learnt on application at the office; and when thus impressed, but not otherwise (for adhesive stamps will not be accepted in payment of the postage), they may be transmitted through the post between places in the United Kingdom under the following regulations:

1. The words 'Post Card' and 'The address only to be written on this side' must be printed on the front of the cards, as in the case of the official post card, the Royal Arms being omitted; but there must be nothing else (the address excepted) printed, written, or otherwise impressed on the face of the cards.

2. Nothing whatever may be attached to the cards.

3. The cards must not be folded, nor may they be cut or in any way altered after they have been impressed with the halfpenny stamp at the office of Inland Revenue.

4. On the back of the cards any communication, whether of the nature of a letter or otherwise, may be written or printed; but such communication must not extend to the front side.

Private cards will not be supplied to postmasters for sale to the public. It must be distinctly understood that no cards, except those which are impressed with a halfpenny stamp at the office of the Inland Revenue, can pass through the post for the postage of a halfpenny if they have anything of the nature of a letter written upon them. There seems to be much misapprehension on this point.

[1] The Postmaster General, in his annual report for the year ending March 31, 1873, says that the permission to allow the public to send in their own cards to be stamped was granted in compliance with the urgent solicitations of the Committee of Wholesale and Retail Stationers of the United Kingdom; but he adds, "of this concession little use has been made".

The regulation set down by the Inland Revenue Office under which postcards brought by the public to be impressed with halfpenny stamps were:

1. They must be white, *i.e.* not tinted in any way.

2. They must be of the same dimensions as the official postcard; viz., 4¾ inches by 2⅞ inches.

3. They must not be thinner than the official postcard; viz., 120 to the inch; nor thicker than the telegraph card; viz., 60 to the inch.

4. The words 'POST CARD' and 'THE ADDRESS ONLY TO BE WRITTEN ON THIS SIDE' must be printed on the face, as on the official post card, but there must be nothing else (the address excepted) printed, written, or otherwise impressed on the face of the card.

5. All cards must be sent in with evenly cut edges.

6. At the right upper corner of the face of the card a space measuring 1¼ inches from the top edge of the card and 1 inch from the side must be left for the stamp, and this space must be free from print both on the face and the underside.

Not more than 10,000 can be received in one warrant.

Not less than 480 can be stamped.

APPENDIX V

THE FIRST AMERICAN POSTCARD

The following notice was issued by the American Post Office Department, dated Washington April 15, 1873:

The necessary appropriation having been made for the purpose, the Department will, on the 1st of May, 1873, commence the issue to Postmasters of the Postal Cards authorized by the act of June 8, 1872.

DESCRIPTION

The card adopted is five and one-eighth (5⅛) inches in length and three (3) inches in width; and is made of good stiff paper, water marked with the initials U.S.P.O.D. in monogram.

The face of the card is engraved on steel, surrounded by a border, in scroll work, one-eighth of an inch in width. The one-cent stamp, printed on the upper right hand corner, is from a profile bust of the Goddess of Liberty looking to the left, and surrounded by a lathe-work border, with the words "U.S. Postage" inserted above and "One Cent" below. On the upper left hand corner are the words "United States Postal Card", with directions to "write the address only on this side—the message on the other". Underneath, and occupying the lower half of the

card, are ruled lines on which to write the address, the top line being prefixed with the word "To". The back of the card, intended for the communication, is entirely plain, being devoid even of ruled lines. In color, the body of the card is light cream; the printing, velvet brown.

No variation in size, shape, color, or in any other particular, will be made from the regular style to accommodate special cases; nor will the Department do any printing on the cards beyond that specified in the description.

PRICES

Postal Cards will be sold for one cent each, neither more nor less, whether in large quantities or in small.

USES

The object of the Postal Card is to facilitate letter correspondence and provide for the transmission through the mails, at a reduced rate of postage, of short communications, either printed or written in pencil or ink. They may therefore be used for orders, invitations, notices, receipts, acknowledgements, price lists, and other requirements of business and social life; and the matter desired to be conveyed may be either in writing or in print, or partially in both.

In their treatment as mail matter they are to be regarded by Postmasters the same as sealed letters, and not as printed matter, *except that in no case will unclaimed cards be returned to the writers or sent to the Dead Letter Office.* If not delivered within sixty (60) days from the time of receipt they will be burned by Postmasters.

IRREGULAR CARDS

An ordinary *printed* business card may be sent through the mails when prepaid by a one-cent postage stamp attached; but such card must contain absolutely *no written matter except the address;* otherwise it will be treated as not fully prepaid, and refused admission into the mails.

COUNTERFEITS

All cards different from those herein described, with postage stamps printed or embossed thereon, and purporting to be U.S. Postal Cards, are COUNTERFEITS; and the manufacture of such cards, or the attempt to use the same, will subject the offender to a fine of five hundred dollars and imprisonment for five years. (Sec. 178, Postal Code.)

SPOILED CARDS

Postmasters will not, under any circumstances, be permitted to redeem or exchange Postal Cards that may be misdirected, spoiled in printing, or otherwise rendered unfit for use, in the hands of private holders.

REQUISITIONS

The Department will not furnish less than five hundred (500) Cards on the order of a Postmaster. Individuals desiring Postal Cards will purchase them of a Postmaster, as in no case can they obtain them upon direct application to the Department.

RETAIN THIS CIRCULAR FOR FUTURE REFERENCE.

E. W. BARBER,
Third Assistant Postmaster General.

APPENDIX VI

POSTAL UNION CARDS

On July 1, 1875, the basic rate for a letter was fixed at 2½d. per half ounce for all member countries of the General Postal Union, and for postcards, at one penny and a farthing, that is, at half the letter rate.

A new postcard of this value was designed, printed and manufactured by Messrs. De La Rue and Company, and although these new postcards were at first marked for sale at 1s. 4d. per dozen, they were subsequently sold for 1s. 3d. per dozen.

This Foreign Postcard was in use only a short time, when it was made obsolete by the issue of two new postcards in 1878 when the Universal Postal Union was established. One card, of the value of ONE PENNY, was for use to countries within class A of the Union, to which the letter rate was 2½d., and the other card of the value of THREE HALF-PENCE was for countries within class B of the Union, to which the single letter rate was 4d. Both cards were designed and printed by Messrs. De La Rue and Company.

Complying with the new international regulations, both these cards were headed

UNION POSTALE UNIVERSELLE

GREAT BRITAIN (GRANDE BRETAGNE)

which caused such strong feelings of resentment in Ireland that a new issue was quickly printed worded GREAT BRITAIN AND IRELAND.

135. Regulations forbade the sending of postcards abroad until July 1875. This postcard is overstamped 'Not Transmissible Abroad' and is dated May 1873. (Reduced)

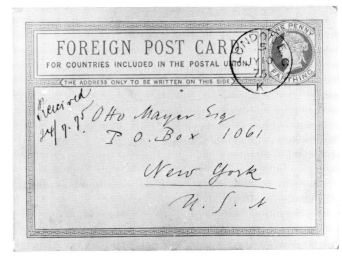

136. The first postcard allowed to be sent abroad. (Reduced)

APPENDIX VII

COMMERCIAL AND OTHER IMITATIONS OF POSTCARDS

Not long after the new halfpenny postcards were issued in 1870, enterprising businesses produced similar looking cards in imitation and distributed them as trade-cards or for advertisement purposes. Some of these efforts copied the design almost to detail, but in place of the Queen's head, there would be a trade mark, or some other depiction. These commercial imitations were persistently used despite orders from the G.P.O. forbidding them. Some foreign countries copied the new postcards very closely, notably Chile, where the head of Colon substituted that of the Queen.

On October 30, 1894, an instruction was given by the General Post Office:

The Postmaster General finds that, notwithstanding the provisions of Section 6 of the Post Office Protection Act 1884, and the notice issued to the public respecting them on the 9th September 1890, Envelopes, Postcards, Money Order, Postal Order, Telegraph, and other forms, as well as date stamps and other postmarks in use by the Post Office, are still frequently imitated for advertising and other purposes.

These imitations are calculated not only to embarrass the Postmaster General's Officers in the performance of their duties, and especially in the treatment of letters, telegrams, and other postal packets, but also to mislead the public, and to cause serious inconvenience and annoyance . . .

The 6th Section of the Post Office Protection Act of 1884 laid down that:

(1) A person shall not, without due authority:

(a)—make, issue, or send by post or otherwise any envelope, wrapper, card, form, or paper in imitation of one issued by or under the authority of the Postmaster General, or of any foreign or colonial postal authority, or having thereon any words, letters, or marks which signify or imply or may reasonably lead the recipient to believe that a post letter bearing the same is sent on Her Majesty's service; or

(b)—make on any envelope, wrapper, card, form, or paper for the purpose of being issued or sent by post or otherwise, or otherwise used, any mark in imitation of or similar to or purporting to be any stamp or mark of any post office under the Postmaster General, or under any foreign or colonial authority, or any words, letters, or marks which signify or imply or may reasonably lead the recipient to think or believe that a post letter bearing the same is sent on Her Majesty's service; or

(c)—issue or send by post or otherwise any envelope, wrapper, card, form, or paper so marked.

Under a fine not exceeding 40s.

Examples of these advertisement cards are extremely scarce, for it seems that few have survived. A tailor, Charles Lynes of Shoreditch, issued one, with the date December 1871 printed on it. It is an exact imitation of the halfpenny postcard, printed in the same mauve colour and with the same sort of ornamental frame. Headed "POST CARTE", there is, instead of the Royal Arms, a monogram of C.L., and in place of the Queen's head is featured a man's head labelled R. TICHBOURNE, in the panel reserved for 'ONE PENNY'. Presumably this is a misspelling of the name Roger Tichborne, the claimant in the famous Tichborne trial, and was used to direct attention to the advertisement. In place of the usual instruction for the address is printed "THE ADDRESS OF THE BEST TAILOR IN LONDON IS ON THIS SIDE", which is followed by a printed facsimile of a handwritten address—

Mr. Charles Lynes,
Everybody's Tailor,
183 Shoreditch, London E.
(next door to the London & County Bank)

On the obverse side is printed a written message drawing attention to Boys' and Youths' overcoats from 8s. 6d.

This could be described as a caricature of a postcard, and is worthy of a place with the famous Mulready caricatures of the 1840s.

APPENDIX VIII

THE FIRST BRITISH PICTURE POSTCARDS

In the first volume of *The Picture Postcard* for 1900 an account is given of an interview with the manager of the London branch in Paternoster Square of George Stewart and Co., the Edinburgh publishers, when the question of the first picture postcards to be printed in the British Isles was discussed.

"The idea of publishing pictorial postcards", he said, "occurred to us after having issued note-paper bearing views, and this idea was put into execution immediately after the postal authorities allowed postcards to be made by private firms. This was in the summer of 1894, and during September we published a set of views of Edinburgh by process blocks, and we followed this up with view-cards of towns in Scotland by lithography. We have customers' invoices dated September 1894, proving that our cards were on sale in the shops during that month, and specimens would doubtless have been shown by our travellers early in September. As the view-cards gradually grew more popular, and other makers' cards began to appear on the market, we greatly extended our series, making use both of lithography and of the photo process blocks. Next we availed ourselves

CLEAN YOUR BOOTS, SIR!

137. An early English picture postcard postmarked June 17, 1895, published by Beechings Ltd., The Strand, London. (Slightly reduced)

of the collotype and the 'three-colour' printing processes, and the sale of our cards of Edinburgh in these styles of production was so great that we turned our attention to London, with the result you see" (referring to a series of coloured view-cards of London).

The next endeavour "was to issue cards of a topical character, that is, having views or portraits of interest at the moment. Our first topical picture postcard was that illustrating the Nile Expedition of 1897. It bore portraits of Gordon and the since famous Sirdar, Lord Kitchener."

Following a further description, the manager described how these first picture postcards were both of court size and the official shape, and bore on the top left-hand corner a tiny view of some public building or interesting place of Edinburgh and environs. It was noticed how similar they looked to the views previously printed on headed note-paper.

It was explained how, since the first specimens were published, Messrs. Stewart issued many other different varieties, including some in the three-colour process, and it was stressed how all their cards were genuine British make, designed and printed by Messrs. Stewart in Edinburgh. Pioneer publishers in London were Messrs. Blum and Degen who, in 1895, produced four cards in the collotype process showing little views of London, and Beechings Ltd., of the Strand, who also in that year issued a set of London scenes coloured partly in red. But there is nobody qualified to be called the first, because as soon as the new regulations came out, printers in nearly every town throughout the kingdom, began to publish picture postcards.

138. One of London's early pictorial cards, 1895, printed in Germany. (Slightly reduced)

(G.P.O. Announcement)
PRIVATE POSTCARDS

On and after the 1st September 1894 Private Cards bearing halfpenny adhesive stamps can be sent through the post under the following Regulations:

The cards must be composed of ordinary cardboard not thicker than the material used for the official postcard. The maximum size, having regard to the variety of forms, must correspond as nearly as may be to the size of the ordinary post-card now in use. The minimum size must not be less than $3\frac{1}{2}$ inches by $2\frac{1}{4}$, and the Cards must not be folded. With regard to the address side, the rules differ very little from those which relate to the Official Cards. On the address side which must bear the postage stamp the sender may add the words "Immediate", "Forward", "Local", and also may attach by gum or paste a small label as at present. Nothing else may be attached on the address side except a postage stamp and on the reverse side nothing but a receipt stamp. The arrangements of course apply to Reply Postcards.

The word "Postcard" on the address side is not objected to.

The infringement of any of these Rules will render the cards liable to letter Postage.

APPENDIX IX

PICTURE POSTCARDS PROHIBITED IN TURKEY

By virtue of a decision of the Council of Ministers of November 14, 1900, an Imperial decree by the Sublime Porte forbade the introduction into, or sale in, the Ottoman Empire, of postcards bearing the names of God and his prophet Mohammed, any pictures of the Kaaba or anything relating to Mecca and other Mussulman religious buildings or ceremonies, as well as portraits of Mohammedan women. As a consequence of this edict, the police in Constantinople seized all such cards found in shops and in the possession of salesmen of Turkish nationality, and bought up all they could find in the possession of foreigners.

This ban, forced on the Turkish people because of deep religious sentiments, certainly struck a blow at a most remunerative trade, for by far the most popular cards pur-chased by tourists were those showing the mosques and religious ceremonies and functions, as well as the interesting souvenirs of Turkish women dressed in their distinctive Oriental costume. In an article written at the time on this subject, the belief was expressed that such cards would become scarce and desirable as collectors' items.

APPENDIX X

INSURANCE POSTCARDS

During 1900 in Germany it was possible to insure by postcard. Anyone receiving an insurance postcard through the post was insured for thirty days against accidents which might befall him while travelling by rail, coach, tram, bus or other vehicle anywhere in Europe. The equivalent of 10s. per week was paid for two months in the case of a simple injury, and, in the event of death, the sum of £50 was paid to the legal heir. In 1907 there was a similar policy available in England, printed on attractive picture postcards for the Ocean Accident and Guarantee Corporation Ltd.

This is the same system which applies today at our airline terminals, when, by inserting the required amount into a slot machine, a stamped postcard is obtained which, after being addressed to the next of kin or appropriate person, is then put into the nearest postbox.

Some very popular series were produced by retouching. Most of the alleged snow-scenes were faked. So were the moonlight views. In order to have postcards showing busy Exhibition scenes on sale when an Exhibition opened it was necessary to draw in the crowds by hand on photographs of the empty avenues.

Sometimes the modifications were only in the caption. For a few years after the death of President McKinley in 1901 there was a good demand for a card showing the Irish home of his ancestors. When his name was no longer topical further reprints described it merely as "An Irish Farmhouse" and "An Irish Kitchen".

Bearing in mind that the postcards were printed far away in Germany, by people quite unfamiliar with the subjects of their skills, some of the mistakes are understandable. Confusion between the beauty spots of Glenariff and Glengarriff, Killiney and Killarney, is inevitable. The transformation of Dublin University from greystone to redbrick was a typical colouring slip. More difficult to explain is a view of Tintern Abbey, on the Welsh Border, labelled as Blarney Castle!

Considering the circumstances it is remarkable that the errors were not more frequent. To find them it may be necessary to scrutinize many thousands of normal cards—probably finding numerous otherwise interesting items during the search.

APPENDIX XI

VARIANTS

Picture postcard collectors sometimes look for some particular aspect. This might be some special subject, or the work of individual artists or selected firms and publishers. One field for study shows how a basic photograph can be modified to yield a wide range of different postcards. There are postcards still being printed in the 1960s from the same originals as first appeared in the 1890s, and intervening issues depict effectively the changing public tastes in brightness of colouring and degree of glossiness.

In some cases an out-dated view has been modernized by deleting a horse and cart and substituting a motor-car. An advertisement card issued by Guinness's brewery changed a row of horse-drawn drays to a fleet of motor lorries.

APPENDIX XII

UNITED KINGDOM POSTCARDS

(Extracted from *The Post Office—An Historical Summary*, published by H.M. Stationery Office, 1911)

Postcards were introduced in Austria on the 1st October 1869, and, authority of Parliament having been obtained, they were first issued in the United Kingdom on the 1st October 1870. They were of one quality only, and no charge was made for them over and above the value of the stamp. The number passing through the post in the year 1871 was about 75,000,000.

In the following year a charge of ½d. a dozen was made for postcards, and private cards were allowed to pass impressed with a stamp by the Inland Revenue Department; the number rose to 76,000,000, fell to 72,000,000 in 1873, but rose again to 79,000,000 in 1874.

In 1875 the stout cards were first issued at a charge of 2d. a dozen, and the charge for thin cards was raised to 1d. a dozen; these rates continued in force until 1889, the annual consumption of postcards averaging about 140,000,000 during this period.

In 1889 the charges for stout and thin postcards were fixed at 6d. and 5½d. respectively per packet of 10 cards, with the result that stout cards began to displace thin cards to the extent of about 18,000,000 a year. The average consumption of postcards for the next five years was about 236,000,000.

From the 1st September 1894 private cards with ½d. adhesive stamps have passed as postcards, and from January 1895 postcards of the "court" size have been issued.

In 1897 the prohibition of writing or printing on the address side of a postcard was removed; and the charge on an unpaid postcard was reduced from 2d. to 1d.

In November 1899 the limits of size were raised to 5½ by 3½ inches; and the issue of oblong stout cards was discontinued.

In November 1905 the price of both stout and thin postcards was fixed at 6d. per packet of 11.

The result of these changes, especially the permission to use private postcards with ½d. adhesive stamps, has been to raise the consumption of postcards to about 860,000,000 in 1908-9 and 866,000,000 in 1909-10.

In 1909-10 private postcards formed about 90 per cent. of the total number of Inland postcards passing through the post.

On 22nd June 1911, the day of the coronation of His Majesty King George V, thin postcards, both single and reply, were placed on sale at the face value of the stamps they bear.

Reply postcards were first issued on the 1st October 1882; their use has not been very extensive, and only 1,657,425 were issued in 1909-10 for Inland use.

Letter cards were first issued in 1892, the selling price being fixed at 9d. for eight. This price remained unaltered until the 22nd June 1911, since which date they have been sold at face value—1d. each. The number of letter cards issued in 1909-10 was 6,057,792.

BIBLIOGRAPHY

The Postage and Telegraph Stamps of Great Britain, PHILBRICK AND WESTOBY. (Sampson Low 1881)
The Mulready Envelope and its Caricatures, MAJOR EVANS. (Stanley Gibbons 1891)
St. Martins-le-Grand, Vols 1-16, *G.P.O. Magazine*
The Picture Postcard, Vols 1 and 2, London 1900-1901, edited by E. W. RICHARDSON
The Post Office, An Historical Summary. (H.M.S.O. 1911)
Uphill, JOHN EVELYN WRENCH. (Ivor Nicholson and Watson 1934)
A Hundred Years of Photography, LUCIA MOHOLY. (Penguin Books 1939)
La Carte Postale Illustrée, GEORGES GUYONNET. (Paris 1947)
The History of the Christmas Card, GEORGE BUDAY. (Rockcliff 1954)
La Poste par Ballons Montés, J. LE PILEUR. (Yvert et Tellier, Amiens 1943)
A History of Valentines, RUTH WEBB LEE. (Batsford 1953)
Seaside England, RUTH MANNING-SANDERS. (Batsford 1951)
Pioneer Postcards, J. R. BURDICK. (Nostalgia Press, New York) Reprint Edition 1964
Pictures in the Post, RICHARD CARLINE. (Gordon Fraser 1959)
The Penny Post 1680-1918, FRANK STAFF. (Lutterworth Press 1964)
Old Prints and Engravings, FRED W. BURGESS. (Routledge and Kegan Paul 1924)
London Tradesmen's Cards of the Eighteenth Century, AMBROSE HEAL. (Batsford 1925)
A Picture Postcard Album, LAUTERBACH AND JAKOVSKY. (Thames and Hudson 1961)

ARTICLES AND MONOGRAPHS

Pictorial Postcards, NORMAN ALLISTON. *Chambers Journal* Oct. 21, 1899
Visiting Cards. *The Queen* Oct 17, 1896
Old Artistic Visiting Cards, ETTORE MODIGLIANI. *The Connoisseur* April 1905
Postal Cards and Covers, Leeds 1900-1901, edited by WALTER T. WILSON
Ansichtskarte, ERWIN MULLER FISCHER. *Postpapyrus zum Postflugzeug* Berlin 1939
Die Erste Ansichtskarte der Welt, MIRKO VERNER. Wiener Briefmarken Spiegel, Feb. 1965
The History of Bamforths, R. M. JONES